PRAYER IN MOTION

CONNECTING WITH GOD IN FIDGETY TIMES

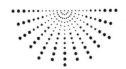

JEFFREY A. NELSON

APOCRYPHILE
PRESS

Apocryphile Press

1700 Shattuck Ave #81

Berkeley, CA 94709

www.apocryphilepress.com

Copyright © 2018 by Jeff Nelson

Printed in the United States of America

ISBN 978-1-947826-82-3 | paperback

ISBN 978-1-947826-83-0 | epub

Please join our mailing list at
www.apocryphilepress.com/free
We'll keep you up-to-date on all our new releases,
and we'll also send you a FREE BOOK.
Visit us today!

For Robert, Virginia, Paul, and Margaret

CONTENTS

ACKNOWLEDGMENTS

At first, I didn't know whether to include an acknowledgements page for this book, because at first consideration this seemed to have the fewest hands involved out of the books that I've written so far.

But then the more I thought about it, I realized that it may have the most.

In part, this book came about as a direct result of my ministry as a pastor. As I mention several times in these pages, I've had so many conversations over the years with members of the congregations that I have served about how busy and overwhelmed they are; how difficult it is for them to maintain any semblance of a balance in their lives among the many obligations that they face on any given day. And, of course, that includes time spent with their church and nurturing their spiritual lives.

I had so many people in mind while writing that it would be impossible to name them all. So I'll just acknowledge the people of Emanuel and Grace. I hope that this book helps a lot of people, but as I wrote I had a hope that it would help you in particular.

Thank you to John Mabry at Apocryphile for the opportunity to birth this idea into book form.

And thanks as always to my family for their love and support.

INTRODUCTION

Without my realizing it, the idea for this book came about during the summer of 1998, between my freshman and sophomore years of college. That first year had involved a tremendous amount of transformation and deepening of my own understanding of faith and my relationship with God, which I wanted to process further over the long break.

Thanks to a friend's dad, I landed a job working in a factory that made egg incubators, where I was assigned to a station that featured a variety of tasks building the parts of the machine that helped control the temperature. I sawed and soldered pipes, attached valves to the larger mechanisms that would limit or increase water flow, and on certain days I had to stack freshly cut pieces of metal to deliver to other stations. I still consider it one of the best jobs I ever had before becoming a pastor.

I brought all the questions and curiosities from my completed school year with me to the workday and wanted to find a way to make the most of what was for the most part a mindless job. With each new fabrication assignment, it took me a few minutes to get down the routine of how to make the item, and then I could allow my thoughts to wander while my hands stayed busy.

My shift started at seven in the morning. After a few weeks, given all that I had yet to digest related to my faith, I decided that, beginning at eight o'clock each day, I would pray. I'd spend the first hour after punching the clock getting situated and figuring out what I'd need to work on for the day, and then at eight I'd address my thoughts to God for a while. Some days these prayers would be general petitions for family and friends; some days they'd focus on certain situations that were weighing most heavily on me; some days they'd be more inquisitive, where I'd ask God about some aspect of God's nature or how God was present in the world.

Before I started my career as a pastor, I cannot recall any other job where I set aside time to pray in the midst of my responsibilities the way I did that summer in the factory. I can certainly name other positions where this practice would have benefitted my approach to my surroundings, but that was the only time when I was intentional about nurturing an awareness of God while engaging in the responsibilities of my workday.

I believe that devoting time and attention to prayer while engaging in my daily work helped integrate my sense of the spiritual with the rest of my life. This is not a new concept, but it was my first instance of pursuing this goal for myself.

There is a good chance that you are reading this because you have a similar goal. You may be wondering where spirituality and prayer fit into a life that is chock full of people, positions, and events for which you are responsible. You know something about the importance of maintaining a connection to God, but don't know how or where to fit it into a schedule stacked with duties to your family, your job, your community, your basic home upkeep, your friends, your hobbies, and whatever else is already calling for your time and energy. Where are you supposed to wedge any kind of spiritual practice into that?

If that wasn't enough, maybe you do finally have a chance to sit down with a devotional book or a Bible or just an absence of noise, and this lack of activity unnerves you. You aren't used to being so quiet; your mind is still racing from a full day. You have excess energy to spend. Is there a way to pray while burning it off? Is that even allowed?

My short answer is yes. But you see that there are many pages after this one, so I plan to expound on why I think that is the case. I plan to show you ways to think about prayer, spirituality, and God that involve the aspects of your life in which you're already steeped. Sometimes we step away for a while to be able to see them, and sometimes we can't step away but we can see them anyway. Whichever is most true, whichever is most manageable, whichever makes the most sense for you at this current juncture in your own life, there is a way to see it. And God, concerned and ever-present, wants you to see it.

As a pastor and spiritual director, I have lost count of the number of times I've been told by people I meet in these contexts how busy they are. Over my years of ministry, I have heard from so many who tell me how much stress they feel, how much they are struggling with trying to achieve some semblance of balance between family and work, how much time they'd love to devote to a faith community or to personal prayer if only there was more time or they could let go of something else. But with wits and calendars already stretched thin, they believe that there is nothing that can be done. Spirituality becomes the item to be cut from the list because there's already too much else.

But what if there was a different way to think about how spirituality relates to the rest of your life? What if we stopped thinking about it as an item on a list and instead approached it as the paper on which the list is written? What if we thought about spirituality as encompassing all of what we do and who we are, and practiced it accordingly?

Again, this is not a brand new idea. Many spiritual teachers and writers have been exploring this subject for centuries. I will give a brief introduction to one whose reflections are most pertinent to what we'll explore here.

Brother Lawrence was a Carmelite monk whose days at his monastery were filled with the most basic and arbitrary tasks, such as washing dishes and sweeping the floor. Rather than grouse about how he'd rather be praying than performing these chores, he opted to transform the chores into acts of prayer themselves. His view, which has been shared by many other spiritual thinkers, is that we cultivate an awareness that God is present in everything that we do, including the most mundane activities that we cannot avoid doing.[1]

In his classic work *The Practice of the Presence of God*, Brother Lawrence wrote, "the time of business[...]does not with me differ from the time of prayer; and in the noise and clatter of my kitchen, while several persons are at the same time calling for different things, I possess God in as great tranquility as if I were upon my knees at the blessed sacrament."[2]

Our lives are full of "noise and clatter," whether in the kitchen, the office, while wrangling children for bedtime, while folding laundry, or a hundred other different things that call for our attention. Brother Lawrence suggested that since all of it is infused with the presence of God, one ought to change how we think about them and prayerfully consider what God is up to with us as we tend to them.

This book is an invitation to such consideration. We each in our busy lives need ways to see how God is within the busyness both when we have time to rest and ponder it, but also in the heart of the commotion. God is concerned with the clamor of our days; let us in turn be concerned with God as we deal with it all.

The first two chapters of this book introduce how to think about this in a general way. Before charging in, it will be helpful to lay some groundwork regarding why we might take this mindful approach to our daily lives. Chapter 1 will reflect more on how we can be mindful of God's presence while active, while

Chapter 2 will offer the theological grounding for how and why God is with us in all things.

After that, we'll explore a series of different activities with which we may be concerned on any given day, as well as ways to practice mindfulness while doing them.

Brother Lawrence will join us again in Chapter 3, as we think about how God is with us as we engage in the basic tasks of household upkeep, such as dishes, laundry, cooking, and cleaning. We will hear more about practicing the presence of God in the "noise and clamor of our kitchen."

Chapters 4 and 5 will deal with similar issues concerning how the physical and spiritual are connected, as the former will explore God's presence with us while eating. The latter will be concerned with caring for the body through exercise, and how paying attention to the various pains, strains, stretches, and strengthening of our efforts can help us become more attuned with how God relates to us as God's created beings.

Chapter 6 will be a reflection on how we fidget to stay engaged at our job or elsewhere through little things, like clicking our pens or bouncing our legs. This chapter will borrow some general principles from the spiritual practice of using prayer beads to explore how such little actions can become times of remembrance and petition to God.

Chapter 7 will show how our morning commute or the long drive to our favorite vacation getaway can be opportunities to lift up prayers to God. It will include some of the elements of spiritual pilgrimage, showing how even the brief times of travel we experience are journeys with God.

Chapter 8 will explore walking as a spiritual practice, whether around the neighborhood or at our favorite park. The practice of using a labyrinth will be our guide. It will also touch on concepts related to communing with God in nature, and how noticing what is around us in the created order can deepen our appreciation for how God is in all of it.

In Chapter 9, we will think about art as a way to express and respond to God's creative inspiration that resides within us. It will be an invitation to reflect on how making art, such as music, painting, pottery, drawing, and poetry, are acts of becoming co-creators with God, partnering with God to bring something new into the world.

Chapter 10 will show how prayer and acts of service are complements rather than adversaries; one informs and enriches the other rather than takes away from it. I've been a part of and seen so many arguments that pit the two against each other, and I believe that this is not meant to be how we think about them.

Finally, Chapter 11 will be our summary and conclusion, serving as a sort of benediction for your own exploration.

I hope that this book starts you on a journey of transforming how you think about the busyness of your days. Whether or not you believe you can currently manage stepping away from the bustle of life in order to make time for God, at least there are ways to think about how God is with you in the noise and clamor.

Whether while building incubators or entering data at a desk, whether while riding the subway to work or driving the kids to music lessons, whether while grocery shopping or washing the car, God is with us in every activity, moving with us. Let's make it a point to respond to that movement.

NOTES

[1] John R. Tyson, ed. *Invitation to Christian Spirituality* (New York: Oxford University Press, 1999), p. 314-5.

[2] Brother Lawrence. *The Practice of the Presence of God.* (Grand Rapids: Spire Books, 1967), p. 30.

BE ACTIVE AND KNOW

I opened the door and set down my bag. The memory of this retreat house, a quaint structure at the back of a sprawling property, had been beckoning to me all week; a place hidden among the trees where those such as myself seeking to lay down their daily demands could do so in silence and stillness. To me this place was holy ground, a welcome haven of retreat and rejuvenation.

I'd visited often enough by that point to have established a routine to which I thought the layout of the building and nearby grounds lent itself. I'd begin most visits on the main floor, my prayer books and journal laid across a coffee table in front of my wicker chair while a fire crackled in the potbelly stove in the corner. I'd spend time in quiet contemplation, allowing my chosen devotional to guide my thoughts while writing some down.

Late morning would bring a time of walking the Chartes-style labyrinth in the adjacent field. I'd watch my feet slowly make every turn as the sun warmed my face and arms until I reached the center, where I'd stop to listen to the birdsong and the wind's gentle rocking of the trees. After retracing my steps back around,

I'd linger for a moment at the entrance, thankful for access to one of my favorite spiritual practices.

After lunch I would move to the upper level, which included a small reading nook where I'd usually spend several hours with a book before recognizing the end of my time. I'd sign the visitor log and make the trek back to my car to return home.

Most visits would have this rhythm. I'd become comfortable with it, and anticipating its familiarity had brought peace even before opening the front door.

Most visits.

I recall one scheduled visit that did not bring this comfort. I'd been agitated the entire way to the grounds, my mind busy with what I'd have to do upon my return. I was making mental lists of people to call and tasks to finish. I was imagining conversations that I dreaded having and developments I would need to catch up on in the next few days. My mind and spirit were jumbled into a knot that arriving at this house could not undo on its own.

Carrying these thoughts with me, I entered as I always had. I pulled out my books and journal, hopeful that I could calm myself through my usual time of prayer. But I was too restless for that, my muscles too tense, my mind too loud. Not even my usual technique—slow breathing with eyes closed—was doing the trick. I had energy to burn, and I needed to move around rather than continue attempting to will myself to sit still.

So I made the labyrinth my first activity of the day instead. At the entrance I offered up a brief prayer for calm to come to my spirit, and then I started walking. Sure enough, every step brought further untwisting, and every movement quieted my thoughts. By the time I'd stepped back out of the space and returned to the house, I was centered for the rest of my time. And it began with a recognition that I needed to pray while moving.

My story comes from a certain place of luxury. I have been fortunate enough to be able to take the time to run off to a retreat center for a day where I can choose to sit in silence, or walk a labyrinth, or sink into a chair and read by myself. I recognize that not everyone is afforded such a privilege for many different reasons.

One such reason is the long list of responsibilities that would confront many who would even try. Your job tasks after a single day off may pile up even higher than usual, to say nothing of the restrictions or hurdles needed to be cleared to get time off. You might need to coordinate with your spouse or partner or with babysitters to watch or drive children to practices and other events. You may not even want to go sit by yourself for a day, choosing instead to do something a little more active like play golf, devote time to a hobby, steal some time at the gym, spend time on the trails of a park, or catch up on household chores.

And yet, because you have picked up this book, I can assume with some amount of certainty that you are also wondering how prayer fits into all of that. If you can't get away, taking time to spend with God might sound like one more item for an already packed to-do list that already has you at the limit of your emotional and physical ability. If you can get away, you'd prefer to move around rather than sit still. When you have time and energy to spend the way you want, being active might sound much more appealing.

Rest assured, the experience at the retreat house that I describe above was neither the first nor the last instance when I've tried to sit down to pray, only to find that stillness was the last thing that I needed, let alone desired. Even when I do manage to calm myself enough to engage in a prayer practice, I may catch myself bouncing my leg, running my thumb along the side of a pen, or even doing something so slight as moving a toe to an unspecified beat. I can be as fidgety as they come.

You may be able to relate, and not just in your own struggle to maintain a prayer life. At work you have those times when you need to get up and move around the office. When reading at home you might tend to drum your fingers on the arm of your chair.

Your morning coffee may be spent standing at the window rather than seated at a table. So you may ask, "If I can't even sit still in these daily experiences, what hope is there for me to take on a spiritual practice?"

There's more hope than you may think. According to a 2005 study conducted by the University of Hertfordshire on children ages 6-8, the students were able to learn better when allowed to fidget with their hands or given chances to move around the room.[1] The same principle is at work whenever we play with our pen at our desk or run our finger along the rim of a glass of tea at home. In lay terms, when we attempt to focus our attention on something, there's a part of our brains that can become bored, causing us to lose our concentration. These small repetitive actions help re-engage that part and give us greater ability to think, process, and remember.[2]

Have you ever felt stumped for an answer to even the simplest of questions or while trying to think of a name? While doing so, do you ever gesture with your hands or click your tongue or tap your hand on a table? These are part of the brain's attempt to jog your memory and help you focus. Believe it or not, your inability to sit still serves a good purpose, and is both natural and common. Perhaps there are ways to work with these human tendencies rather than against them; to redeem them rather than force ourselves to change.

RETHINKING "BE STILL AND KNOW"

I have three reasons for writing this book. One or more of these reasons may also be why you are reading it.

First, I want you to know that it's okay that you can't sit still. As noted above, the felt need to move, to get up and walk for a while, to fidget, is built into our biology as a way to keep our minds active as well as our bodies. Maybe in the past you've attempted a spiritual practice and thought you were doing everything right: you found a great book to guide you, you set aside space in your house and time in your day to sit, but when the moment came you couldn't get your mind and body to cooperate no matter what you tried. It may be that this conception of prayer is not for you. That doesn't make you wrong, nor does it make you incapable of praying in general. It just means that something other than that style of spiritual engagement is more suited for you.

But your problem might not be a matter of nervous energy or a desire to move around. It may just be that your days are packed with tasks, from family appointments to job responsibilities to household chores to community obligations. By the time all is quiet in the evening, you just want to watch a little TV before falling off to sleep and starting over in the morning. Even the idea of fitting prayer into such a schedule just makes you more exhausted. Again, this is normal and common and many more people than you realize have the same issue. And again, you need a more creative way to think about spiritual practice that speaks into your busyness rather than adds to it.

That leads to the second reason: I do think that there are ways to incorporate prayer into the teem and tumble of our daily lives without tacking an additional item to your to-do list or injecting even more anxiety into your already hectic day. I think that there could be a different way to think about prayer that infuses it into everything that you're already doing and that works with your demanding days rather than against them or that makes them even more demanding.

Prayer should not be a burden. The very thought of it should not fill us with anxiety or dread because we think it can only be done a certain way, and that way happens to make us feel like a failure whenever we attempt it. Rather, it should instead be a source of peace, comfort, reassurance, and awareness that God is with us no matter what is happening. As such, rethinking how to do it in a way that makes sense in the context of our lives seems more worthwhile and constructive than trying to shoehorn ourselves into something that doesn't fit no matter how hard we push.

And that brings us to my third and final reason. I believe that whatever we face in a given day has a spiritual dimension. Most of it may not seem like it; many people are used to spirituality being relegated to what happens in a church or a retreat center, or it has to have the Bible or a member of the clergy or some explicit religious symbolism involved in order for it to "count." You may not be used to thinking about how driving your kids to school or dealing with a difficult coworker or putting clothes in the washing machine or sweating on your elliptical machine are related to spirituality. Again, we've been conditioned to think that once all of that is finally done, we can focus on something spiritual like prayer or reading a devotional or attending a worship service.

I want to suggest to you that your busy day is full of opportunities to engage the spiritual, and that God is related to everything you do at home or at your job or at the YMCA or while sitting in the stands at weekend soccer practice. And as you know, these settings and activities don't tend to feature silence and serenity. The question then becomes how we engage the spiritual aspect of these times and places, nurturing our awareness of God in their midst rather than waiting until they're finished.

Thus far, I have been skating around the main objection to this idea. So often, those who advocate for greater attention to spiritual practice (often including myself, I admit) encourage those seeking to tend their prayer lives to step away from the busyness, to sit and rest and recharge and block out the noise. One may hear the phrase to "be still and know" who God is, citing this phrase from Psalm 46:10 to make their case.

I certainly would not deny that taking time to be still and know is a worthwhile method to observe prayer, centering, and meditation. As I note at the beginning of this chapter, I try to do this when I can, whether at my home, my church, or at other treasured places of retreat. But I sometimes have too much nervous energy to be still, or I'm facing down a full day's worth of planning, meetings, and interactions with others. And if the frantic lives of those around me—my neighbors, my congregation, my colleagues, my family, and my friends—serve as a good representative sampling (which I suspect they do), many others struggle to reconcile a desire to be more faithful to spiritual engagement with the reality of life's daily demands.

People can tell us to "be still and know" as often as they wish, but all the well-meaning reminders in the world won't remove the stress and anxiety of family and work. It won't magically create blank spaces on the calendar or cancel activities at which we're expected. Maybe, then, it is time to think about alternatives to this idea, and infuse our busyness with a prayerful sense of God with us instead.

What might change if we choose to view the many tasks of our day as opportunities for spiritual practice, rather than adversaries to it? What if we prayed at our desk or at the kitchen sink or in the stands during T-ball, recognizing that God is concerned for all of it? What effect would that have on how we see the world?

FOCUSING IN THE WILDERNESS

As I have already observed, we are beset by distractions on all sides. Our lives are filled with things that distract us, that demand our attention, and that make taking on a regular routine of prayer difficult. And whether we admit it or not, whether we are proud of it or not, whether we would claim them or not, we each have our own ways of coping with the stress that fills our day. We each have ways to "get through it" that help take the edge off.

We may tell ourselves that these things help us focus, but it may be more accurate that they help numb us, serving as brief moments of pleasure in an endless sea of anxiety. For one person it may be food, for another caffeine or alcohol, and for yet another, spontaneous purchases or pornography or the Internet. These may bring relief and focus for a moment, but many of our coping mechanisms, habits, and addictions can lead to physical, emotional, and spiritual sickness rather than health or wellness. What we might claim provides temporary clarity can instead do lasting damage.

Jesus faced his own set of distractions in Matthew 4:

> Then Jesus was led up by the Spirit into the wilderness to be tempted by the devil. ²He fasted forty days and forty nights, and afterwards he was famished. ³The tempter came and said to him, "If you are the Son of God, command these stones to become loaves of bread." ⁴But he answered, "It is written, 'One does not live by bread alone, but by every word that comes from the mouth of God.'" ⁵Then the devil took him to the holy city and placed him on the pinnacle of the temple, ⁶saying to him, "If you are the Son of God, throw yourself down; for it is written, 'He will command his angels concerning you,' and 'On their hands they will bear you up, so that you will not dash your foot against a stone.'" ⁷Jesus said to him, "Again it is written, 'Do not put the Lord your God to the test.'" ⁸Again, the devil took him to a very high mountain and showed him all the kingdoms of the world and their splendor; ⁹and he said to him, "All these I will give you, if you will fall down and worship me." ¹⁰Jesus said to him, "Away with you, Satan! for it is written, 'Worship the Lord your God, and serve only him.'" ¹¹Then the devil left him, and suddenly angels came and waited on him. (Matthew 4:1-11)

Jesus is driven by the Spirit out into the wilderness, where he fasts for 40 days. Let's go right ahead and reject any attempts at over-spiritualizing this: the text says he was starving. The elements have worn him down, he is exhausted, his lips are dry and cracked, his limbs are weak, and his stomach feels like it is on fire from hunger. This is as far from being a fun time at summer camp as you could get.

We can also assume that he did not just sit in one spot for the entirety of his stay. We can picture him on an ongoing search for water sources, or taking shelter in caves during storms or the heat of the day. Did he pray? We can deduce that he did, given that he does so later in the Gospels. But given the context of his situation, such prayer might not have taken place for long stretches at times — it could have been offered while on the move, or perhaps he observed it while continually aware of the pangs in his stomach and the prickle of the weather against his skin.

But if all of the natural and biological struggles weren't enough for him, Matthew tells us about three specific temptations that he faced. Let us set aside for the moment questions about who the devil or tempter is and instead devote our attention to what he is tempted to do.

In the first instance, Jesus' adversary takes aim at the easiest and most obvious: he's famished. The pitch starts with, "If you are the Son of God..." In other words, if you have this special relationship with and connection to God, you're fully capable of feeding yourself. So go ahead and turn a few stones into a nice little meal for yourself. Jesus resists by quoting scripture, "[humanity] does not live by bread alone, but by every word that comes from God." So far, so good.

The tempter then whisks Jesus up to the highest point of the temple in Jerusalem, and begins the same way: if you have this special relationship with God, go ahead and jump and God will protect you. Again, Jesus answers with scripture: "Do not put God to the test." Okay, that's two down.

We're told about one last shot. This time the tempter presents Jesus with all the kingdoms spanning the world. All earthly power can belong to Jesus if he does one simple thing: he can bow down and worship this adversarial being. So much good he could do with this level of power, the difference he could make! But this final time, Jesus again answers with scripture: "Worship and serve only God, and no one and nothing else."

We can parse out what Jesus is tempted to do in these three instances and find parallels to today. But notice the common thread that weaves through Jesus' answers: all three times, he remains focused on God. No matter what comforts are offered to him as potential distractions, his attention doesn't waver from his understanding of who God has called him to be and what God has called him to do. These opportunities to use that calling for his own benefit represent something other than that, and he refuses to be sidetracked by them.

Given these explicit examples, we could apply them to his entire time in the wilderness. Not only could he have been distracted by satisfying his hunger, testing God's protection, or claiming conventional earthly rule, he also could have done so by finding other forms of relief from his 40-day sojourn through heat, cold, wind, rain, hostile animals, weakness, despair, boredom, and so much more. But if what we're told is any indication, he remained focused on God no matter what else presented itself.

The distractions in our lives are constant, palpable, demanding, and draining. The ways we seek relief, self-medicate, or tell ourselves we have some semblance of control are just as numerous and their effectiveness may vary. Is it possible to travel through the grind of our daily schedules with an understanding that God is with us every step of the way? What could change if we developed a focus on God at the expense of all distraction and temptation, moving through each activity prayerfully rather than frantically?

Just as God called Jesus to remain focused, so does God call us in the same way. Rather than hope for a free moment when we can try to give ourselves to a spiritual practice apart from the elements swirling around us, perhaps we should also think about ways to claim our time in the wilderness as a spiritual practice itself.

BEFORE WE GO ANY FURTHER

I will return to this point later, but it may be that you picked up this book with an objection in mind. Or perhaps this objection arose once you began reading. I don't want you to get the wrong idea about what I am presenting. I certainly would not want you to think that I believe sitting still is inferior to the active sort of prayer I will focus on over the course of this book. Quite the contrary: I have found great meaning and benefit in forms of prayer that call for slowing down, sitting in silence, and engaging in quiet mindfulness and reflection.

But there come instances when, like the story that opens this chapter, I cannot quiet myself the way those forms require. The vast majority of the time, I'm unable to get away to a place of retreat to observe them. Many days I can't even find time to practice them in the routine of my daily schedule. If I, a pastor and spiritual director, have trouble doing this, I can safely bet that many others with their own hectic work and family lives do as well.

That said, however, I am also a believer in caring for oneself in appropriate and fulfilling ways and in making time for winding down from the busyness of the day. So while I will focus on how to integrate prayer and contemplation into a variety of activities where life typically will not allow you to slow down, I would not argue that the fast pace to which you may be accustomed is the only speed at which anyone should operate.

What I am saying instead is that God is a part of the fidgeting, the running around, the things that keep us moving and that sometimes fill us with nervous energy such that we couldn't sit still even when finally presented with the opportunity. Those things have a spiritual side, and tapping into that can be life-giving and affirming.

But don't mistake that for a call to never rest or relax or even attempt forms of prayer that call for being still and knowing God in quiet centering. Slowing down to recharge, caring for oneself away from life's demands—these are essential to physical, emotional, and spiritual health. We each must tend to that for our own vitality, and no amount of demands on our time should steal any and every chance to do so. Whatever works best for your own renewal in this way, give it proper attention.

Meanwhile, I want to help you know God during the active times. Because—make no mistake—God is there, too.

PRAYER EXERCISE AND QUESTIONS FOR REFLECTION

1. Whatever you use to keep track of your daily obligations, set it before you on your lap or on a table. This could be a day planner, a desk calendar, or an app on an electronic device. Take a minute to look over everything listed for the next day, followed by the next week. After doing so once, go back to the beginning and read through it again, this time at a slower pace.

2. Take time to notice how each item makes you feel. Does an upcoming event make you feel anxious or scared or joyful or sad? Try to identify why it causes this reaction. Is this an activity that pops up routinely? Does it make you feel this way every time?

3. Take time to picture the people you will see at each activity, or what you will have to do to consider it completed. What is each step involved? What will be the intended outcome? How will it help you or others?

4. Read through your activity list once more, this time offering each of them to God. As your eyes land on each item, go through the following series of prayers. First, name the event itself: "God, I lift up [this activity] to you." Next, name the feelings you identified earlier and what is causing them: "God, I am [nervous/angry/happy] about this because…" Next, pray for others who may be involved: "God, be with this person because…" Finally, pray for a sense of God's presence during the activity, no matter what it might involve. Conclude by thanking God for always being near.

5. As you journey through these activities on your schedule, take time to notice the ways God might be with you as you do them.

NOTES

[1] "Fidgeting children 'learn more,'" BBC News, April 12, 2005, http://news.bbc.co.uk/2/hi/uk_news/education/4437171.stm, accessed March 29, 2017.

[2] Jessica Hullinger. "The Science of Why We Fidget While We Work," *Fast Company,* March 24, 2015. https://www.fastcompany.com/3044026/the-science-of-why-we-fidget-while-we-work, accessed March 29, 2017.

2

ENGAGE RATHER THAN RETREAT

*I*n the first chapter, I told a story about visiting a retreat house. I also admitted that only a certain cross section of people can afford to do such a thing due to the constraints of their families, jobs, or finances. And yet many spiritual resources tend to present running away for a day, a weekend, a week, or even longer as the norm for being able to experience God's presence to the fullest of our ability. It makes sense: to escape for a while to a remote location, leaving all conventions and responsibilities of one's life behind for a time, might provide the best opportunity to listen for God and finally hear what God has been trying to say amid the din of our many other activities.

As mentioned, getting away is not a realistic possibility for most. Doing so would involve an incredible amount of preparation and permission from family members and bosses that might add to one's stress level rather than relieve it. Even the prospect of such a time of retreat can be daunting, especially when cross-referenced with one's daily or monthly calendar. Maybe there's a free space on the horizon a few months from now, but who knows what might come up between now and then?

Aside from such logistical hang-ups, going on retreat to experience God's presence assumes that such a presence either is not in the midst of one's regular and mundane activities, or is impossible to decipher without proper guidance from a guru during a special time set apart in a far-off place.

I do not mean to downplay the usefulness of such spiritual guides or retreats. If one can manage getting away, such times can be valuable encounters and provide tools for clearer discernment of God's activity in daily life. And trained companions such as spiritual directors or clergy are ever available for personal appointments and sessions, whether in a retreat setting or in a meeting at their office or a coffeehouse. These resources can be meaningful, important, and informative.

However, absent the time and money needed for such things, what is the alternative? Are there ways to be more attentive to God in the everyday without all this extra planning?

To help us with this question, we turn to a story about Jesus on a mountaintop.

THE MOUNTAIN IS TEMPORARY

Six days later, Jesus took with him Peter and James and John, and led them up a high mountain apart, by themselves. And he was transfigured before them, [3]and his clothes became dazzling white, such as no one on earth could bleach them. [4]And there appeared to them Elijah with Moses, who were talking with Jesus. [5]Then Peter said to Jesus, "Rabbi, it is good for us to be here; let us make three dwellings, one for you, one for Moses, and one for Elijah." [6]He did not know what to say, for they were terrified. [7]Then a cloud overshadowed them, and from the cloud there came a voice: "This is my Son, the Beloved; listen to him!" [8]Suddenly when they looked around, they saw no one with them any more, but only Jesus.

[9]As they were coming down the mountain, he ordered them to

tell no one about what they had seen, until after the Son of Man had risen from the dead. (Mark 9:2-9)

This story about Jesus is in three of the four Gospels in the New Testament, and even has its own special name: the transfiguration. It begins with Jesus taking only three of the twelve disciples up a high mountain (maybe the other nine couldn't afford the retreat registration fee). He doesn't seem to let on about what this little side trip is about, but they find out in short order when Jesus' appearance undergoes a dramatic physical change—a brilliant vision of white and light overtaking what was there before. And if that wasn't enough, two of the great prophets of Israel's history, Moses and Elijah, appear with him.

This display might be amazing, but for the three disciples it is also terrifying. In his fear, Peter manages to stutter out a suggestion that he and his friends construct three dwellings for Jesus, Moses, and Elijah. As if to help indicate that this is the wrong take on the situation, a cloud descends on the entire scene, out of which the divine voice speaks: "This is my Son, the Beloved; listen to him!"

More than once in the Bible, people have incredible experiences of God on mountains. Moses and Elijah are included in that group, among others. These accounts have helped inspire the term "mountaintop experience," meant to describe a special moment where one has a revelation of some kind that lends great clarity and direction to one's life. These don't often happen on mountains in actuality, but they are impactful enough. For people of faith, they are inspired by God.

For Peter and the others, the impact of this moment is evident in his stated desire to mark it for prosperity through the building of dwellings. What better way to commemorate a life-changing experience than to erect some sort of permanent structure? This way, these three, along with the others who couldn't make the trip, could return to this spot whenever they wish to pray, reflect, and maybe seek a whole new mountaintop experience. Whenever they have some free time, they can take a day or more to seek retreat and respite in this sacred place.

But as the voice in this story indicates, setting aside this little piece of geography for future getaways isn't the point. The takeaway of this mountaintop experience is clear: "this is my Son... listen to him!" Then the disciples depart, heading back the way they came, away from the peak and back to the base where most of their time would be spent among the area villages and its people, its hustle and bustle, its commerce, its demands, its needs.

Even as they returned to the busyness of travel and interaction, they were to listen to Jesus. It would have been much easier to stay in the irenic setting of the mountain. They wouldn't have had as many distractions or responsibilities or interruptions and could have heard everything Jesus wanted to tell them unhindered. But the mountaintop is not where most of life is lived, and it is not the only place where God is speaking. If it was, then only a select few would ever have the opportunity to hear the voice speak.

Mountaintop experiences are wonderful, and when they come they can be life-altering. But those experiences aren't reserved just for times and places set aside solely for special listening. God is speaking where we live our lives. Cultivating ways within ourselves to listen at home, at work, and wherever else our daily schedules take us is more important than saving up time and money to get away from it for a while, because God is just as concerned with that everyday struggle as we are.

MAKING THINGS OBVIOUS

Carol Zaleski tells the story of a church's worship service during which the pastor had a group of first graders positioned in the front pew as part of their preparation to receive their first communion in a few weeks. He climbed down from his perch at the front of the sanctuary to address the children directly. As it happened, the designated text for the day was the story of Jesus' transfiguration.

The pastor began asking the kids questions about the story in simple and gentle terms. Having been trained in their responses before this moment, they were able to follow his lead with ease, answering questions about where Jesus and the disciples went, who appeared with Jesus during the story, and so on.

After concluding his light quizzing, the pastor then turned to the rest of the congregation and began to address them by saying, "The disciples were obviously astonished to see Christ in glory standing next to Moses and Elijah." As he continued, one girl in the front row raised her hand and asked, "What does 'obviously' mean?"[1]

Before anyone can get to a point where what God is saying seems obvious, we would benefit by breaking things down to more basic understandings of how to listen. As in the case of this story, even the meaning of the word "obvious" might not be all that obvious when it comes to paying attention to God's voice and presence in our lives. The notion that God is waiting to be discovered not just on mountains or during retreats but also in the busyness of our day might sound nice, but it is not all that obvious. Is God really with people as they stare at Excel spreadsheets or try to convince a 6-year-old to get dressed for school or jog on a treadmill first thing in the morning? Why would God care about those moments, and how could one begin to listen during them?

This is why faith communities and leaders have developed spiritual practices over the centuries. They believed that there is something to find—and that is worth finding—underneath our daily experiences, even those we consider the most mundane and unimportant. But often, as in Zaleski's story, what some might consider obvious is not often so for many others.

It is easy for anyone to say that God is everywhere all the time, as many faith traditions claim. One may believe that on an intellectual level, where we have it repeated to us over and over in sermons, books, guided meditations, podcasts, and other media. But in the thick of things where there are bills to pay, meals to cook, commutes to endure, deadlines to satisfy, and general life balance to pursue, bringing that claim to life involves an intentionality and awareness that takes more than verbal repetition of an abstract idea. We need it to become a realized part of our daily world.

And so such practices were born: ways to pray, ways to interact with God and other people, ways to connect one's sense of the spiritual to the rest of our lives. And sometimes heading off for a special time away to hit reset and seek a mountaintop experience is feasible. Or, we can set aside time at the beginning or end of the day to take stock of what the day may hold. But if we can't manage even that, many of these practices are adaptable to our needs.

But what is the point of a spiritual practice? Why pick any of them, if they seem to be so difficult for people to observe? We have them because they help us move God's presence from a static theological concept into the tangibility of our lives. We call them "practices" because regular use of them over a period of time helps change how we view what is happening. To practice is to do something again and again until one becomes better, until an action or way of thinking becomes more natural and less work. When we engage in regular practice of a certain form of prayer or awareness-building, we learn a sort of habitual way of seeing God in all that we do.

While I was going through my program to become a spiritual director, we were each required to observe the Spiritual Exercises of Ignatius of Loyola, a priest who became the founder of the Jesuit order. Each person in the program did so with a spiritual director of their own, and the Exercises themselves involved going through a 30-week-long period of daily prayer, meditating on many events of Jesus' life recorded in the Gospels, weekly meetings with our directors to reflect together, and, if we were inclined, journaling about our experiences.

As I journeyed further through the Exercises and through the program in general, I noticed a shift happening within me resulting from this intensive time of prayer and study. I recall one moment that stands out when these changes were made especially clear to me.

I was at home with my daughter during one of my days off. She was less than a year old at the time, but already able to walk and move around on her own a little. On this day, she became agitated about something I wouldn't let her do and she started working her way into a full-blown tantrum as we both stood in the kitchen. Trying to get her to calm down seemed a futile exercise, and I could feel my frustration mounting as I tried to remain firm while also attempting to diffuse her anger.

Just as I was preparing to put my foot down regarding the entire matter, a voice from within said, "She really needs you right now." This simple statement from somewhere in my spirit helped me to step back and to see my daughter's difficulty in expressing herself at such a young age. I was able to stop and consider that not being allowed to do what she wanted to do was only part of why she was upset. It wasn't that specific thing itself, but rather her discovery of and development within the world she was still trying to figure out. In this way, I could see her more through God's eyes: this fragile, beloved creature who needed to be understood rather than yelled at. This realization helped calm me down so that I could in turn help her, as the internal voice said I needed to do.

I do not think that I could have had that ability to reconsider this situation from a different angle if it hadn't been for the regular spiritual practice that I had been observing up to that point. Such a practice had helped me cultivate a new habit to see even this small and routine parental moment in a new way. This experience for me helped bring the oft-spoken statement about God being everywhere into concrete reality.

At this point, the reader may still wonder how to use such practices if one has trouble sitting still or carving out the time to do them. While the rest of this book will cover that question in various ways, here is something to try the next time you're at your place of work, your home, in the grocery store, or at the DMV or a sporting event or a concert or the Humane Society.

Just look around. Notice the other people who are there. Notice what they are doing, how they are interacting with and reacting to one another. Try to see the little things like facial expressions or how people phrase something they say or the intonations with which they say it. Consider where you are in general and why some may enjoy being here and others may not. Think for a moment about what any one of them seems to need, beyond a price check on a box of cereal or for the line to move faster as they try to get a beer at the concession stand. Before undertaking this exercise, consider whether you have ever thought about such things before? Have you ever thought about how God may be present with the exhausted employee, the embarrassed parent, the angry customer? And why might you be reacting to them the way that you are? What's happening inside of you that causes you to feel annoyance or sympathy?

Spiritual practices, observed over time, help us answer these questions. They help us listen for God's voice at the foot of the mountain. They show us a more dynamic divine reality that we wouldn't be able to see otherwise. And there are a variety of ways to observe these practices, including while we're doing these mundane things, because that's when such an ability to listen matters the most anyway.

I'm a big music fan and love listening to a variety of styles and artists. For a while, I subscribed to a music magazine that would help me keep up with established bands that I liked, as well as discover new ones to try out. I received an issue every month and was able to read up on the typical sort of content that you'd find in such a magazine: concert reviews, artist profiles and interviews, and reviews of new albums.

The first year or so that I received it, there came a point where I could only read each issue for so long before I had to put it down and do something else for a while. I tended to lose interest because after so many pages, every article started to sound the same. The magazine was staffed by talented and capable writers who would try their hardest to describe the music they were reviewing, either by comparing it to similar bands, talking about songs having a certain "flavor," or using a bevy of adjectives in the hopes that the reader would gain a better understanding through the printed word of what something sounds like.

These writers did their best, but in the end music is meant to be heard rather than read about. One can only do so much to describe an experience to someone else; a person really needs to listen for themselves in order to form an opinion. This magazine seemed to realize this after a while and began including a sampler CD with each issue so that subscribers not only could read about the music but experience it in its intended way.

Imagine Peter, John, and James trying to describe what they saw and heard on the mountain to the other disciples. Imagine them using what they thought were their most vivid and descriptive words to try painting this picture for others. Think of moments when someone has tried to describe a time that you can tell was full of meaning for them, but something is getting lost in the translation from speaker to hearer. This becomes even harder when all we have to go on are written words preserved to convey the wonder of the original witnesses. Something more is needed.

In general, spiritual practices are to be experienced and not just read about. They are meant to help cultivate an awareness of God's presence within an individual; a capacity for listening to God's voice amid one's many other obligations. Such practices make this presence and voice more obvious over time, creating space not just at the top of the mountain but down where life actually happens, not apart from the noise but within it.

PRAYER EXERCISE AND QUESTIONS FOR REFLECTION

1. As encouraged above, pick a time when you're engaged in some scheduled activity: grocery shopping, sports practice, dinner with the family, time at the gym. It may even be helpful to choose something before that activity arrives, and prepare yourself to take on this exercise intentionally.

2. Before departing for your chosen activity or before entering the room to begin it, say a small prayer for God to help you listen to God's voice for the duration of the event. Take a few deep breaths to open yourself to what you may hear.

3. Even if you have certain responsibilities during this activity, be intentional about noticing what is happening beyond your own tasks. How do others seem to be feeling about being there? What do you notice about others' moods? What is the overall sense of the event: happy, sad, hesitant, boring, urgent, preoccupied with something beyond this moment?

4. Take time to notice what all of this is causing within you. What do you feel as you speak to or notice others? Is something making you anxious or joyful or disappointed? Why are you feeling this way?

5. What do you think God might be trying to say through your own emotions, or through those of others? What needs seem to be present that God might want to meet in some way?

6. After the activity has ended or after you have completed your part in it and are able to leave, ask God to further show you

how God was present. Say a prayer of thanks for God being concerned about even these routine times.

NOTES

[1] Carol Zaleski, "Virtues of Knowing." *The Christian Century* (October 18, 2011), online, accessed August 31, 2017.

3

WHILE DOING CHORES

*S*hoveling snow makes me grumble.

    I have lived my entire life in Midwestern states, so you'd think I'd have become used to this inevitable and necessary task at some point, but even at this stage of my life, when we've had a hard enough snowfall and I realize what I have to do, I do so with a scowl on my face. I trudge to the door to pull on my boots, heavy coat, gloves, hat, and scarf—I say "trudge" because every step toward the door takes quite a bit of willpower—I head outside to find the shovel hanging in the garage, and I set to work. And I mutter at this intrusion to my day.

At least, I mutter at first. I've found a method of shoveling that works for me where I walk the width of the driveway, my shovel acting as a kind of plow in front of me, each mini-stroll ending with a final scoop of what I've collected into the grass.

There comes a point during this task that I set into a rhythm and my mind can turn its thoughts to other things. I almost forget that I'm out in the cold and I let go of my annoyance at what I have to do. I begin thinking about my family, situations at my church, what I have to do the rest of the day, people I haven't seen in a while, places that have been meaningful to me and how long it's been since I've been back, the current highs and lows of my favorite sports teams, or some piece of pop culture whose meaning I haven't figured out yet or want to finish watching or reading sometime soon. I sometimes even take a moment to appreciate the beauty of winter: the way the snow clings to our tree branches or the way the sun glistens off of it in our yard.

Some of these topics are just for my brain to keep itself occupied while my body finishes what it has to do. Others, however, bring a deeper sense of worry, gratitude, joy, or relief. When I think about how I need to help my son through a school-related issue, or what I might say when I call a church member about their sick relative, or what it feels like to me when I can return to our beach vacation spot or my favorite retreat space, my ruminations take on a prayerful quality. I may be out there for the practical purpose of making sure we can get in and out of our driveway with little trouble, but I'm also using the time to sort through parts of my life that I hope improve or that I'm glad to have or be a part of, expressing silent concern or thanksgiving as I do so.

When I reach the end of the driveway, I look back up at the house and appreciate the cleared space that will allow us problem-free passage between the garage and the road. I take a moment to have a little pride in the work put in toward a job complete. And someplace deep inside where maybe not even I can sense it, I say a prayer of thanks for a physical duty also becoming a spiritual practice.

IT'S NOT ALL CANDLES AND INCENSE

If you're anything like me, chores are not your favorite part of the day. And yet they are as necessary as they are irritating. You need clean dishes off of which to eat, clean clothes to wear, a clear driveway in the winter and grass of reasonable length in the summer, and trashcans that aren't overflowing. We each have different ways of approaching these responsibilities; a different timetable that we've negotiated with ourselves and our households as to when each should be addressed so as not to become overwhelming. For many, some of these are constant, near everyday tasks, especially if you have many living under one roof. Others can allow things to go longer in between running the dishwasher or emptying the laundry hamper.

Some really do enjoy these things. For them, there's a good feeling that accompanies a trimmed lawn or fresh clothes folded and hung. One can look at a list of items checked off and pat oneself on the back, or justify sitting back on the couch to relax later. Still others find it important to help out a busy and stressed family, and this can be an act of love—a way to lift a burden off of someone else's shoulders. So let's acknowledge those among us who like the performance of the jobs for their own sake.

For the rest of us, however, the source of our annoyance at having to do them could be boiled down to one root cause: they take time away from something else. Spending the minutes or hours that these needs demand means that we're not spending it on a beloved hobby, the aforementioned time reclining on the couch, or, for the purposes of this book, time for prayer. When I have to shovel snow, I may chafe at the cold temperature or groan about the physical exertion, but I'm more upset that time spent doing that could be spent in other ways, even if it's nothing at all.

Many chapters in the remainder of this book ask the question of how our time can be reclaimed for spiritual practice. How can we take the time that these chores require and use it to gain greater clarity, direction, and consciousness in our relationship with God?

We may not be able to redeem how we feel about doing them, but we can divert our mental and spiritual energy toward something more productive and meaningful, where we reflect on how God is with us even as we vacuum the carpet or clean the bathroom. God is with us in these small everyday tasks as much as God is a part of crises or celebrations where such an awareness is a greater or more obvious need. If we can focus ourselves to prayerfully consider God's presence, we are able to find meaning in what seems meaningless. And if we are able to find God while using detergent and brooms, we may have an easier time finding God in hospital rooms, while tending to a fractured relationship, in times of financial strain, or while joining another in their happiness or experiencing our own.

God is with us all the time, including the time when we wish we were doing something else. But teaching ourselves to see that involves a change in our outlook and attitude.

LET'S CUT MARTHA SOME SLACK

There is a brief passage in the Gospel of Luke where someone seems to be chastised for doing chores rather than using that time to show devotion to Jesus. Even in just these five verses, there's more going on than we may first realize.

> Now as they went on their way, he entered a certain village, where a woman named Martha welcomed him into her home. [39]She had a sister named Mary, who sat at the Lord's feet and listened to what he was saying. [40]But Martha was distracted by her many tasks; so she came to him and asked, "Lord, do you not care that my sister has left me to do all the work by myself? Tell her then to help me." [41]But the Lord answered her, "Martha, Martha, you are worried and distracted by many things; [42]there is need of only one thing. Mary has chosen the better part, which will not be taken away from her." (Luke 10:38-42)

In a nutshell, this story seems to portray the struggle that this entire book is trying to address. On the one hand you have Martha, who always seems to be on the move preparing, acting, and rushing around. On the other hand you have Mary, lounging at Jesus' feet, taking time to rest and listen to him. By the end of the story, it looks like we're meant to side with one over the other, favoring the one intentionally stopping to pay attention to Jesus over the one in constant motion. Who are we to argue with Jesus, after all?

I imagine more than one reader wanting to do just that. Does Jesus really want us to sit at his feet all the time while the dishes and laundry pile up? Are we really meant to take time for prayer while the dust bunnies gather under the furniture and dinner needs to be made and the length of the grass in the front lawn becomes ever more of an embarrassment? There are real practical issues at stake if we read this as a call to always neglect our chore list in favor of candles, incense, and devotional books. If that is really what Jesus wants us to do in this story, many might give up before they even begin.

A closer consideration of this short passage reveals more complexity. First, it immediately follows Jesus telling a story about a certain Samaritan who helps a man left for dead on the side of the road. His final words after telling it are "Go and do likewise." That becomes important, because here it might seem like he's changed his mind to "go...and stop and listen instead." Many of Jesus' stories and teachings in the Gospels are calls to action; to serve God and others rather than focus only on rituals, traditions, rules, or first checking the credentials of those who need our help. That larger context informs what Jesus is talking about in this story of the two sisters.

And then there's Martha herself, who thanks to this story has been made the Patron Saint of Workaholics. The popular portrait of our saint is of one with rubber gloves, an apron, her hair pulled back, a broom in one hand and a feather duster in the other with one eye on the stove and the other on the sink filled with dishes. We may picture her running through the house straightening pictures and chastising people for not putting their cups on coasters before rushing the kids into the minivan to get to baseball practice or gymnastics.

But is Martha misunderstood? Does she really deserve all the projecting of our own issues with busyness onto her; to be both our saint and our overworked scapegoat? After all, she's trying to play the role of the proper host; one might think that that's of utmost importance when the guest is Jesus himself. She is preparing food, getting all things ready for her visitor, but the task list is so overwhelming for her to do alone that she just wants a little help from her sister. Who could fault her for that?

The answer lies in how Jesus addresses what Martha and Mary are doing. While addressing Martha, he says, "you are worried and distracted by many things." The Greek word for "distracted" is *perispaomai*, which means to draw away or divert something.[1] To be worried and distracted is to be drawn away from what is more important. Her problem, as Jesus characterizes it, is not that she is wrong for trying to show proper hospitality. Instead, what is tripping her up is being distracted by it, missing why she is going through such preparation, all the while becoming frustrated by Mary's lack of assistance.

Martha's hands and feet are busy, but they are the only parts of her body at work. Her ears, eyes, mind, and heart are numbed to the interruption that Jesus himself is providing. The present moment and the opportunities it brings by Jesus being with her are being missed in favor of the moment for which she believes she is faithfully preparing. Such busyness even with the best intentions can bypass why that work is being done.

Jesus does not imply that what Martha is doing is wrong. She's just distracted; her attention is drawn away from God's presence toward her own busyness and resentment. Mary recognizes that Jesus being here is important and is commended for choosing "the better part."

The tendency for many who read this story is to pit Martha and Mary against each other; to frame it as the busybody against the contemplative, as if only one position is important. But Martha wants to properly welcome her guest; her problem is missing who her guest is and why she is going about her important tasks. Jesus implies that there is a way to choose "the better part" while going about one's work. His words suggest that there is a way to fulfill basic obligations of maintenance, cleaning, and cooking without one's attention being diverted.

In other words, there is a way to do chores and sit at Jesus' feet at the same time.

PRACTICING THE PRESENCE OF GOD

I first mentioned Brother Lawrence in the introduction, where I shared a brief quote from his work, *The Practice of the Presence of God.* He both modeled and provided encouragement for others to find God in the little things of each day, which for him included his assigned tasks at his monastery, whether washing the dishes after meals or sweeping the floor. He equated finding God's presence in these moments with receiving the Eucharist during Mass, noting that such was possible in every instance regardless of circumstance.[2]

Practicing such an awareness takes time and patience, as Brother Lawrence acknowledged, and yet it is possible for anyone and everyone. In his writing, he offers several tips for doing so. Among them is the suggestion to begin any activity with a simple prayer to help you become intentional about finding God in the present moment: "Those who set out upon this practice let me counsel to offer up in secret a few words, such as 'My God, I am wholly Thine. O God of Love, I love Thee with all my heart. Lord, make my heart even as Thine'; or such other words as love prompts on the instant."[3] Most people can probably use more contemporary language than in his example, but with a similar purpose of pursuing a connection with God at the heart's level.

We are easily distracted, even in the mind-numbing tasks of

household maintenance. Offering a prayer such as what Brother Lawrence suggests can remind us that these activities have a spiritual dimension, as difficult as that may be to believe. As with any new habit that we wish to develop, redeeming the time that we spend on these responsibilities as moments infused by God's presence may not come easy for us at first, and even such an opening prayer may be hard to remember to do. It may even seem like one additional task that we must remember to do.

However, the more often we begin such activities with such prayers, the more this awareness we are pursuing will move from conscious to subconscious; from intentional to natural. We become less distracted by what we're doing, as with Martha, and more apt to attend to God with us as we envision ourselves as gracious and grateful hosts. We attain what Brother Lawrence calls an "Unclouded Vision," where our whole lives become one continuous act of prayer.[4]

Both Jesus with Martha and Brother Lawrence in his monastery wish to teach their hearers or readers that you're never really too busy to notice God around you. You don't have to wait until evening after the kids go to sleep or when your chore list is done. You don't have to first straighten up the kitchen before finally being able to sit at Jesus' feet. Rather, the nighttime routine of settling the family down for bed and the wiping down of the stove are themselves moments to consider what God is doing.

God isn't waiting for you to be done with those things before you can get down to the more important business of devotion and divine communion. Instead, we can transform our distraction to unclouded vision as we attempt to pursue the "better part" of continuous prayer even in these in-between times that, as it turns out, very much matter to God.

Theologian Richard Lischer recounts his experience as a pastor in his first church out of seminary, a small Lutheran pastorate in rural Illinois. It was so rural, in fact, that there was no garbage pickup in his part of the county. The solution to this issue was a big barrel at the corner of his property where he or his wife would drag their trash to be burned. They may have seen this as an inconvenience at first, but it didn't take long for both of them to see this exercise in a different light—as an opportunity to be out in the midst of a beautiful landscape to watch the sun set while their waste slowly broke down in the barrel's flames. Before long Lischer and his wife would vie for who had the privilege of going to take care of this task.

For Lischer's part, he'd pray for individual people or think about next Sunday's sermon or just reflect on life in general. He even gave this little place a proper name: The Sacred Burning Barrel. It became a place of quiet contemplation rather than just a place to burn trash.[5]

When we learn to "choose the better part" over our own distraction, the mind-numbing obligations of shoveling snow and washing dishes and disposing of garbage become sacred. They become one more opportunity to see God as an active part of our lives at all times. Pursuing this unclouded vision leads to continuous prayer that extends to all that we do. Rather than wait for the right opportunity in our day to finally sit down with God, approaching our chores in this way transforms them into that opportunity instead.

PRAYER EXERCISE AND QUESTIONS FOR REFLECTION

1. Take a few moments to reflect on what household chores you need to do today or within the next few days. Choose one that you really need to do in the next 24 hours. How do you usually view or approach this activity? Does it bring you any joy at all, or do you only see it as an inconvenience to what you'd rather be doing?

2. Before beginning this chore, take time to say a quick prayer. It doesn't need to be very long. You only need to ask God to

remove the distractions and help you focus on God's presence as you complete your task.

3. As you move through doing your chore, think about what God is doing. Think of this in terms of rings encircling each other, each one larger than the last. How is God a part of this activity? How is God currently a part of your life? Your household's life?

4. Who or what do you need to pray for as you finish your task? How do you or others need healing or assurance? What cause do you or others have for celebration? Name at least a few out loud or silently.

5. As you conclude your task, think about how you just spent your time and how it may have been different from past instances when you had to do this. How can you help yourself remember to approach this and other chores in similar fashion in the future, in order to pursue the continual consciousness of God's presence?

NOTES

[1] Matthew L. Skinner. "Luke 10:38-42, Exegetical Perspective," from *Feasting on the Word Year C Volume 3*. (Louisville: Westminster John Knox, 2010), 265.

[2] Brother Lawrence. *The Practice of the Presence of God*. (Grand Rapids: Spire, 1967), 30.

[3] *Ibid.*, 80.

[4] *Ibid.*, 82.

[5] Richard Lischer. *Open Secrets*. (New York: Doubleday, 2001), 65-6.

4

WHILE EATING

*H*ave you ever noticed how many rituals you observe on any given day? I don't just mean rituals related to your prayer life. In fact, the vast majority of rituals that we keep have nothing to do with religious belief (although that could change given the purpose of this book). What I mean by "ritual" is any routine set of steps that you make it a point to take in any aspect of your life.

Here's an easy one. Think about what you do when you wake up in the morning. Maybe when your alarm goes off, your first act is to hit the snooze button and either doze off or lie there resting for a few more minutes. Then your alarm once again raises its irritating tones declaring that bonus sleep time is over, at which point you either hit it again (or several more times, perhaps to the annoyance of your spouse or partner) or you finally succumb to sitting up or rolling out to begin the day. This may lead you to the bathroom, where you do any number of things such as brush your teeth, give yourself a first-time glance in the mirror, relieve your bladder, and so on. Then maybe it's to the closet to pick out work clothes, or to the coffeemaker, or to the refrigerator to search for breakfast, or down the hall to make sure any children who need the early bus are stirring. And on the ritual goes.

We may also have rituals for work such as what procedures to follow for different office tasks. We have rituals for family gatherings, such as who brings what, and certain traditions are always followed when everyone is together. And just as we have rituals for the morning, we also have rituals when attempting to settle back into bed in the evening.

Some rituals we anticipate and treasure, others we endure or accept as "just the way things are," at least until some life circumstance changes.

Have you ever noticed how many of our rituals involve the preparation, serving, and eating of food? Have you ever thought about how often food serves either as the centerpiece or augmentation of our routines, whether just as a one-time function or as a continuing time of gathering that we're a part of?

The aforementioned wakeup routine involves coffee and either a sit-down breakfast or a pre-packaged pastry on the way out the door. The morning staff meeting always has a plate of muffins on the table. Perhaps you have a standing weekly lunch with a group of friends or coworkers. Your regular dinner ritual is either a time of making it a point to sit down together as a family or yet another anticipated evening of heating up a frozen meal before running back out the door for music lessons or T-ball games. Pre-bed rituals may feature a long-awaited glass of wine or a bowl of ice cream.

Such food rituals are more obvious at larger family gatherings. Maybe the holidays feature certain dishes made from special recipes handed down for generations. Perhaps everyone notes that one or more members have food allergies that need to be accounted for. Maybe Grandpa is always the one who cuts the turkey or Uncle Calvin always runs the grill or Aunt Janine always hosts.

My grandparents' entire week was one long food ritual.

Having spent a decent chunk of every summer at their house while growing up, I had the routine down pat. First, the mid-Sunday meal was always a more formal feast, usually featuring pot roast or chicken with assorted sides, and then "dinner" that same day was popcorn or cereal. Tuesday lunches were always a special melted cheese sauce that required a generous amount of butter over crackers. Thursday was Spaghetti Night, which was always odd because my grandma hated spaghetti. Friday was always a field trip to a fast food restaurant.

Before every evening meal, there was always the same blessing:

> Dear Heavenly Father, thank you for this food.
> Bless it to our health and strength.
> We ask in Jesus' name, amen.

While both my grandparents have passed on, on the increasingly rare occasion that that side of the family is gathered for a meal, we say this blessing in part to thank God for the meal but also to remember them.

THE PASSOVER RITUAL

Sometimes we observe food-related rituals for family reasons or health reasons. At other times, it's to explicitly remember what God has done or is doing now. We have few better examples of that than when the treasured feast known as the Passover was established in the book of Exodus:

> The Lord said to Moses and Aaron in the land of Egypt: [2]This month shall mark for you the beginning of months; it shall be the first month of the year for you. [3]Tell the whole congregation of Israel that on the tenth of this month they are to take a lamb for each family, a lamb for each household. [4]If a household is too

small for a whole lamb, it shall join its closest neighbor in obtaining one; the lamb shall be divided in proportion to the number of people who eat of it. ⁵Your lamb shall be without blemish, a year-old male; you may take it from the sheep or from the goats. ⁶You shall keep it until the fourteenth day of this month; then the whole assembled congregation of Israel shall slaughter it at twilight. ⁷They shall take some of the blood and put it on the two doorposts and the lintel of the houses in which they eat it. ⁸They shall eat the lamb that same night; they shall eat it roasted over the fire with unleavened bread and bitter herbs. ⁹Do not eat any of it raw or boiled in water, but roasted over the fire, with its head, legs, and inner organs. ¹⁰You shall let none of it remain until the morning; anything that remains until the morning you shall burn. ¹¹This is how you shall eat it: your loins girded, your sandals on your feet, and your staff in your hand; and you shall eat it hurriedly. It is the passover of the Lord. ¹²For I will pass through the land of Egypt that night, and I will strike down every firstborn in the land of Egypt, both human beings and animals; on all the gods of Egypt I will execute judgments: I am the Lord. ¹³The blood shall be a sign for you on the houses where you live: when I see the blood, I will pass over you, and no plague shall destroy you when I strike the land of Egypt. ¹⁴This day shall be a day of remembrance for you. You shall celebrate it as a festival to the Lord; throughout your generations you shall observe it as a perpetual ordinance. (Exodus 12:1-14)

This set of commands that God gives to the Israelites is a food ritual. God makes it very clear from the start that this will not be a one-time observance, but rather something that they will do every year to remember what God is about to do for them. This ritual will be their way of telling this story from now until the end of time.

First, God gives instructions for the type of lamb to be selected for the main course. It could be a sheep or a goat, but beyond that it must meet a certain set of criteria: a year old, devoid of blemish, and to be divided in proper portions for everyone in the household. And for those households who can't afford a lamb on their own, they can go in on one together with their neighbors.

Next, we have the instructions for preparation. At twilight on the 14th day, everyone is to slaughter their lamb and get it ready to be cooked. A little of its blood must be smeared on the doorposts and header of their doorways to spare them from the angel of death.

Next, we have the instructions for cooking. The lamb—all of it, including the head and inner organs—is to be roasted on an open fire. Any other form of preparation such as boiling or leaving it raw is unacceptable. In addition, they must prepare certain side dishes, namely bitter herbs and unleavened bread. Why unleavened? Because they won't be able to wait around long enough for the yeast to cause it to rise.

Finally, we have the instructions for eating. The long and short of it is that this will not be a meal meant to be savored. Everyone should be fully dressed, including sandals on their feet and walking staffs in hand, and they need to eat as fast as possible. This is for the same reason as going with unleavened bread: they need to be able to get up and go at any time due to what is about to happen. God is about to do something awful (let's not minimize that part of the story), but also something wonderful. God is about to set the people free from their collective life of slavery and oppression and deliver them into a new way of being God's people, but in the short term it's going to involve a need to leave in a hurry.

As mentioned, these instructions come with a command to keep this ritual every year long after these events pass. By doing so, the people of Israel will not only remember this story but re-present it. They won't just talk about the meal that their ancestors ate, they'll actually eat the same thing that they did just before God liberated them from their oppressors. Israel's descendants will embody this experience all over again by sharing the same food together as when this ritual was first established.

In this way, those who eat this meal together will not just keep remembering what God once did, but also what God continues to do. Through rituals like the Passover for Jews and the sacrament of communion for Christians, people of faith have opportunities to remember that God's presence is still very much active among them and not just crystallized in stories from long ago. Such rituals, particularly those that center around the sharing and eating of food, remind us that God not only saved once, but keeps saving; not only loved once, but is still loving; not only led once, but is still leading.

REMEMBERING GOD DURING OUR OWN FOOD RITUALS

The first method of incorporating a prayerful attitude into eating that may come to mind is including a blessing before meals. Much like the brief grace my grandparents said every evening, this may be the quickest and easiest way to acknowledge God as part of your eating. But as with any prayer exercise, doing this can quickly become a rote exercise. After a while it loses its effectiveness, because you may no longer think much about the words that you say, especially if you use the same words every night.

Perhaps there is a way to think about prayer before meals that can keep it from becoming a mindless activity to which you give cursory attention before picking up your silverware. One may reframe it as a point of entry rather than a formality; an invitation to remember God's presence throughout the meal, much like the Passover meal was meant to do for the Israelites. One could change the general wording of pre-dining prayers to say, "We are not only thankful for what has been prepared and for those who prepared it, but we, too, prepare to receive God's Spirit through the enjoyment and sharing of this food, and open ourselves to how God may be revealed as we partake together."

When is the last time you can remember savoring what you were eating? When can you recall last thinking about how your food tasted; how it felt as you took another bite and began chewing? While eating, have you ever stopped to consider that your food is a gift, either as something picked, packaged, prepared, or served by someone else or as a source of nourishment and energy? If you've never thought of your food that way, how do you think such contemplation might affect the pace at which you eat, or what you think about while you eat?

Such questions have the potential to bring us more fully into the moment of eating. Our consideration of the answers helps us remember that food is a blessing, and it may shift our thoughts from what we need to do after we finish our meal toward the potential for enjoyment in the present moment while we eat. By asking such things while eating, we may be able to slow down and acknowledge how God is with us now, in the present, rather than in the past or future only.

I try to pay attention to issues related to digestion. Crohn's Disease is a part of my family's health history, so when I feel a bit of discomfort I worry about its cause. I sometimes let my imagination get away with itself and envision a doctor's visit where I am finally given the news of my own diagnosis. Such concerns have led me to be vigilant about such matters, including the intentional scheduling of regular checkups and procedures that help me monitor my health in this way.

Through consultations with my primary care doctor and digestive health specialist that have included some deductive reasoning, I've found that stress often plays a role in intestinal discomfort. Knowing this about myself has also helped me address it in productive ways. But rather than continue to share some of my health issues with you, let's move on to talk about health in general.

You see, I am not unique. The causes of problems such as Irritable Bowel Syndrome have been linked to high levels of stress.

The more anxious you are, the higher probability that your body will have physical symptoms. This is because we have a high collection of nerve endings in our stomach and digestive tract. When our brain is on high alert, it sends messages to our gut that cause it to react in unpleasant ways, which is why when we're nervous our stomachs get upset and in the worst cases we have to rush to the bathroom to empty things out one way or the other.

An article from the Institute for the Psychology of Eating (did you know there was such a thing?) observes that there's a correlation between the speed at which we eat and how well our bodies digest and absorb food. Author Emily Rosen writes:

> During survival situations, evolution has figured out a way to re-route all of our metabolic energy away from the midsection and direct it to arms, legs, and head for quick fighting, fleeing and instinctive thinking. You don't need to be digesting your jellybeans when you're fighting for your life. It's a total waste of metabolic energy. Conversely, the beauty here is that when we're nice and relaxed, the parasympathetic nervous system literally switches on full, healthy, and empowered digestive and assimilative function.
>
> So the point is this – if you're eating under stress, your digestive capacity is weakened. Blood flow to the gut can be four times less, enzymatic output in the gut can be 20,000 fold less, activity across the intestinal villi is decreased, and nutrient excretion is accelerated.[1]

In other words, when we're rushing through a meal in between meetings or between getting home from work and hurrying the kids out the door to evening activities, our brains send messages to our bodies to route most of our energy and attention to places other than our digestive functions. On the other hand, eating in a slower, more relaxed state of mind will cause the stomach to relax and do its job more thoroughly.

All of this is to say that the way our minds process our immediate surroundings and respond to stimuli affects our physical health. When the mind is stressed, the body is stressed.

Most prayer practices call for a time of calming both mind and body in order to properly set the tone for both to go through the exercise. They begin with sitting comfortably in quiet spaces, usually with a time of deep breathing. Why do such practices encourage this? Because to most fully experience these times of spiritual centering, we must first ensure that our mental and physical selves are relaxed enough to receive what the practice is meant to share.

Conversely, when we end such periods of prayer, many practitioners report feeling more at peace, both inwardly and outwardly. They return to their lives a little calmer than before. A regular discipline that sets aside time for these exercises has the potential to form new habits of relating to oneself. This leads to the reduction of stress in the mind, which in turn lessens stress on the body.

In other words, the physical, mental, and spiritual are all connected. As tempted as we might be to separate these into different boxes—physical care over here, then mental health over there, and maybe spiritual attentiveness if we find time—the whole of our selves suffers. One inevitably affects the others in positive or negative ways.

Transforming our times of eating to be slower and more relaxed and approaching our food as gifts to be received can help us become more attentive to God in the moment, as well as more attentive to our physical needs. In that sense, not only does the food we eat become a blessing, but the way we consume it becomes a blessing as well. Keeping this in mind can deepen our eating rituals and help us remember and live into their spiritual dimension.

PRAYER PRACTICE AND QUESTIONS FOR REFLECTION

1. As you sit down to eat your meal, take time to think about who has prepared it and how long it may have taken. If it was someone other than you who cooked, pause to express appreciation for the work they put into making it.

2. Whether it is customary or not for you to say a prayer before eating, at least take time to invite God into this time. In addition to thanking God, ask God to be an active part of your receiving this food into your body.

3. As you eat, notice the smells, tastes, and textures of your meal. Chew and swallow at a slower pace to savor each bite and to think about how you will use its energy for the next part of your day. Think about how each mouthful is a gift that you will need between now and when you eat next.

4. As you finish, pause again to thank God and those who prepared the food. Rather than hurry away from the table, rise slowly as a continuation of acknowledging the blessing of this time that God has helped provide.

NOTES

[1] Emily Rosen. "2 Powerful Tips for a Powerful Digestion," Institute for the Psychology of Eating, online, accessed September 15, 2017.

5

WHILE EXERCISING

*E*ver since I was in seminary, I've been trying to be more conscious of my health.

In those days, I had taken to eating McDonald's a couple times a week, including as a late night snack. I was drinking soda and alcohol just as often. I largely stayed away from vegetables and fruit. And the rigors of graduate school had me frequently sitting somewhere reading and writing without a lot of physical activity.

This potent combination of poor eating and a sedentary lifestyle added up to a lot of weight gain. But it also brought the potential for worse physical problems given my family's health history, which includes heart issues, diabetes, cancer, and Crohn's disease. Aware of this, I made multiple attempts to change what I was doing to my body.

Those years featured a lot of false starts and good intentions. Multiple resolutions to watch my eating and head to the gym usually petered out after a week or two. I've since recognized that food is one of my go-to methods of self-comfort. I experienced quite a bit of stress in those days, and that's why I found it so easy to rationalize another fast food run or another evening drink.

My last semester of school, I decided to stop playing around with my health. I forced myself to go to the gym 3-4 times a week, I cut out fast food completely, and I severely limited the amounts of soda and alcohol that I consumed. My goal was to lose 20 of the 35 "seminary pounds" I'd gained by graduation, and to my delight I was able to hit it. It was a wonderful feeling, and I wanted to keep that up as best I could.

I've had better seasons than others over the years regarding this ongoing commitment. The times immediately after both my kids were born stand out in particular, as well as other major transitions that required me to figure out a new life rhythm. They were also times when I'd seek out comfort food as my coping mechanism for the added stress, so I tended to dig myself into a hole.

In recent years, I've become much more of a runner. Let me just say that I don't really enjoy running. I still have awful memories of gym class in junior high, when the designated activity of the day was running a mile around the school. Even so many years later, that experience still has some part of my brain convinced that I am not a runner. My preferred method of cardio since my seminary days has been the elliptical machine: it's easier on the joints and placates the fearful eighth grader within me still holding firm that running is not now, nor will ever be, my thing.

I've been doing my best to fight back against my subconscious on this. I sometimes supplement my elliptical training with jogs around the neighborhood or on a treadmill. Thankfully, the former has conditioned my breathing so that I'm not wheezing after a few minutes, and I can do a few miles with little problem, even if the last stretch can still be a bit trying.

For years I've wanted to sign up for a 5K. I want to show the past self within me that something like this has always been possible if ever I'd buckle down and put in the effort. In fact, I sometimes wonder how many of these I could have done over the years if I hadn't waited until my late 30s to get serious about it. I've now run several 5Ks, with some of them bringing minor sprains that have taken me back to the elliptical machine instead of the treadmill.

Even besides the issues of health and self-confidence that influence my exercise, there's also something spiritual about it. I am very aware of my body during my workouts: my muscles straining and moving, my breathing and heart rate as I get further into my routine, my aches and pains, the natural cleansing process of sweat, the need for rest, rehydration, and nutrient replenishment after. I've become more in touch with my body through running and other forms of exercise, having established a much better relationship with it since those first few months of striving before seminary graduation.

I'm now at the point where I need to exercise, because I want this relationship with my body to continue. I enjoy the health benefits, the self-assuredness, the spirit-body connection that it forges.

FINDING THE TIME

Just as I did my final year of seminary, we may become aware of our need for more physical activity. We may be motivated due to our family's health history or a diagnosis of our own. We may be seeking an outlet for blowing off steam at the end of a long day of responsibility. We may do it for our own self-confidence, or as a way to be around others with similar goals. We may be alarmed at how winded we get just by walking up a flight of stairs or after even a brief time of playing with our kids.

Unfortunately, finding time to exercise can be just as difficult as finding time to pray. Many people may decide that they're finished before they even start due to looking at their daily schedule and throwing up their hands at how little time there seems to be to get in a quick workout. We may worry that making time for exercise will mean sacrificing something else, and none of the other things on our to-do list seem negotiable.

And yet, none of that makes our desire to establish a better relationship with our bodies go away. What can we do? And how can prayer be a part of our exercise?

In an article in *Entrepreneur*, business owner Josh Steimle explains why he makes exercise a regular part of his day, even sometimes at the expense of his work:

> If exercise stops, then my health goes downhill. With the loss of physical health my productivity at work goes down. I become depressed. I lose motivation to do the things that make my business successful. I've learned firsthand that excellence in one area of my life promotes excellence in all other areas of my life. Exercise is the easiest area of my life to control. It's easy to measure. Either I get it in, or I don't. When I do, it lifts up all other areas of my life, including my business.[1]

Steimle recognizes and names the connection between physical health and his performance in other aspects of his life. Having a good relationship with your body, listening to its needs, and giving it the nourishment and activity that it requires improves your ability to think, work through problems, engage tasks with full attention and creativity, and approach everything with more energy and stamina.

All the same, this may be difficult for us to rationalize or to make time for. Some of our reasons may be more practical, such as access to facilities, financial affordability, or a work or family schedule that is more unbending than that of people in positions like Steimle's. For others, we may believe that the schedule is more unbending than it is in actuality, out of fear that budgeting time to tend to our own health will take time away from something else, which will cause us to feel like a lazy or negligent worker, partner, or parent.

As with any practice, spiritual or otherwise, making the time to do what we can is the first step. Exercise involves intentionality, whether it begins as getting up for a walk a little earlier than you otherwise might roll out of bed, heading to the YMCA over your lunch break, or signing up for an evening class while the rest of the family is occupied with other activities. Like prayer, exercise involves establishing new habits. Once you get that far, you can deal with the rest.

BEING MINDFUL WHILE EXERCISING

Maybe you've already figured out how to incorporate exercise into your day, and the above encouragement to get started isn't a strong factor. The next question is about the relationship between exercise and prayer, whether how that relationship actually is or how it could be. The answer to this has two parts: the relationship between body and spirit, and how to tend to that relationship while working out.

To address the first part, we turn to a passage from Paul's first letter to the Corinthians:

'All things are lawful for me', but not all things are beneficial. 'All things are lawful for me', but I will not be dominated by anything. [13]'Food is meant for the stomach and the stomach for food', and God will destroy both one and the other. The body is meant not for fornication but for the Lord, and the Lord for the body. [14]And God raised the Lord and will also raise us by his power. [15]Do you not know that your bodies are members of Christ? Should I therefore take the members of Christ and make them members of a prostitute? Never! [16]Do you not know that whoever is united to a prostitute becomes one body with her? For it is said, 'The two shall be one flesh.' [17]But anyone united to the Lord becomes one spirit with him. [18]Shun fornication! Every sin that a person commits is outside the body; but the fornicator sins against the body itself. [19]Or do you not know that your body is a temple of the Holy Spirit within you, which you have from God, and that you are not your own? ²⁰For you were bought with a price; therefore glorify God in your body. (1 Corinthians 6:12-20)

In this passage, we meet up with Paul in the middle of an argument. In this part of his letter, he even quotes their words back to them as part of his counter-argument. "All things are lawful for me," they say, meaning that they're interpreting God's grace as a permission slip to do whatever they feel like: all things are lawful because God will just keep loving us and provide forgiveness if we ask for it after the fact.

Among other things, the Corinthians are using this rationale to use or abuse their bodies in certain ways that satisfied their desires but were not honoring the physical selves with which they were entrusted. They are indulging in food practices that are harmful either to them or to others who still cling to the tradition of their Jewish heritage, and they are abusing the divine gift of physical intimacy by soliciting prostitutes.

Paul calls for a different way to think about the body, which is rooted in its being created by God. "Your body is a temple of the Holy Spirit," which harkens back to the second creation story in Genesis 2 where God literally breathes life into the first man. We are still full of the breath of God's Spirit, houses of the holy, and such a temple needs proper tending and honoring.

Paul follows this up with an even bolder claim: "You are not your own." The Corinthians seemed to think that their bodies were a disposable possession that they could do what they wanted with so long as it could remain functional. They compartmentalized the physical and spiritual into two different spheres, failing to consider that they are related and that how we treat one affects the other. To care for the physical is to care for the spiritual, because the physical is just as sacred; just as beloved by God because God made and provided it to begin with.

To put an even finer point on it, the Greek word for "body" in this passage is *soma*, which can also be translated "self." For Paul, one's body was an integral part of who a person was; it couldn't be separated out in favor of one's mind or soul. Rather, one's body made up the self as much as those other things. To care for or abuse one's body was to do so to one's self.[2]

When we think about this in terms of exercise, tending to our bodies means tending to these houses of God's breath that we have been given and with which we have been entrusted. Even if we aren't consciously praying as we run or lift weights, we are engaging in a deeper relationship with the physical aspect of our God-gifted selves.

Writer Mette Ivie Harrison explains this in her own way:

> As a writer who sits on a computer and types away in imaginary worlds, having conversations with imaginary people, it would be an understatement to say that most of the time, I am not in touch with my body. But when I run, I can't help but feel every step, every jolt, every pain. And that is a glorious thing. It's not pleasure, but a sense of being alive.[3]

Harrison's description of what running means to her could be applied to any form of what is usually called "body prayer," that is, engaging in prayerful communion with God through moving your body and being attentive to what it's doing and how it feels. There is no one form of physical exertion that this could apply to. This could include paying attention to the movement your arm makes or the tinge of pain in your hand when you strike a heavy bag during a martial arts workout. It could involve feeling the breath move in and out of your lungs during a cardio workout. It could involve hearing and feeling every connection that your feet make with the ground during a morning walk or jog.

As Harrison describes, body prayer involves being present to your muscles, joints, bones, and organs; claiming what they feel as part of yourself, whether you are struggling to push it to a new limit or finding what you're currently capable of doing as you begin a new routine. Many try to zone out during their workouts via their earbuds or by clicking on one of the many TVs around most fitness rooms. Engaging one's body prayerfully invites us to remain aware of what our physical self is doing, how it feels, and what it can do.

You could call me an "anxious sleeper," if that's a thing. I've made many visits to the dentist in recent years because I've cracked both my lower back molars due to grinding at night (I also wear a bite guard now). Some mornings I'll wake up with aches in my shoulders and neck due to sleeping in a strange position or because I carried too much stress with me to bed the evening before.

A couple weeks ago, I started to think about how to address the stiffness and soreness more intentionally. Since my seminary days, I'm always on the lookout for tweaks that I can make to how I care for my body; even though I'd long been attempting to remain faithful to an exercise routine, I decided to add a short morning ritual to loosen up my joints and muscles.

And so, upon waking (and even before coffee), I'll come downstairs, fill my water bottle, and do sets of stretches that target my shoulders, torso, calves, and thighs. They're seven stretches in all, and I do three sets of each. The improvement to my flexibility was almost immediate, and instances where I wake up with the stiffness that prompted it are now quite rare.

I now look forward to this early morning stretch time. Usually at least one cat joins me; sometimes I put on some reflective music, and I sip my water as I go. The whole routine doesn't take longer than 5-7 minutes, but it has become a treasured part of my day.

This time has taken on a prayerful quality. I do each stretch slowly and deliberately, and make it a point to notice how my body feels as I reach and move. I focus on the physicality of the action rather than think about the day's to-do list or otherwise let my mind wander. All my attention is on what I'm feeling, where I'm especially hurting, what might need more care or patience.

I call this time prayerful even if I don't engage in active acknowledgement of God. Such acknowledgement is more implicit as I deepen my relationship with this earthly vessel of mine, this piece of clay into which God has breathed and given life. I come away with a greater understanding of who I am as a created being and how to tend to myself in faithful ways.

I feel a responsibility to do what I can with what I've been given; to be a good steward of these muscles, bones, and sinews as best I can.

There is a certain liturgy to what I do. I know which exercise comes after which. I am familiar with the movements and transitions, my own individual "work of the people." And I come away with a consciousness that Spirit and flesh have met in this space.

Perhaps I should even conclude with an "amen."

PRAYER PRACTICE AND QUESTIONS FOR REFLECTION

1. If you already have a workout routine, how much conscious thought do you give to how your body is feeling as you do it? If you do not, how could you make time to do even 20 minutes of movement a day, or a half hour several times a week?

2. Before you begin your workout, say a short prayer, such as, "I give thanks for this temple, this part of myself." Acknowledge that your body is a divine gift that God created and that you are meant to steward as you are able.

3. During your exercise, notice what your body is doing. What specific parts of your body are moving, how are they moving, and how do they feel? Feel the breath go in and out of your lungs, your quickened heartbeat, the sweat gathering on your skin. Think about how many different parts of your physical self are making this workout possible.

4. After you've completed your workout, notice where you are

sore, what parts still need to calm down after exerting so much energy. Say another short prayer similar to the one said before you began, such as, "Thank you for this part of myself, and what I am able to do with it."

NOTES

[1] Josh Steimle. "Why Exercising Is A Higher Priority Than My Business," *Entrepreneur*, April 22, 2015, online, accessed September 26, 2017.

[2] J. Paul Sampley, "The First Letter to the Corinthians," from *The New Interpreter's Bible, Volume X* (Nashville: Abingdon, 2002), 862.

[3] Mette Ivie Harrison, "I Feel God When I Run," *The Huffington Post*, August 12, 2015, online, accessed September 28, 2017.

WHILE CLICKING YOUR PEN

*W*hen I was in 5th grade, I joined the school band. As in most districts, this was my first opportunity provided through the school to learn an instrument and join an ensemble, and I decided that I wanted to join the percussion section. Because we were all still learning how to play in general, each section would have its own rehearsals a few times a week, in addition to the entire band figuring out how to play together.

As we began preparing for our first concert in front of parents and others, our teacher directed us in a few songs chosen for our ability level, one of which included a snare drum solo. Why I felt so motivated to volunteer for this is lost to me, but I decided that I wanted to be the one to play this part, and I made my wishes known to our director with perhaps more enthusiasm than I needed to show. Sure enough, I landed the solo.

The entire part consisted of a simple repeated series of eighth and sixteenth notes for ten or twelve measures, which for a 5th grader would be a big deal even though to more experienced drummers it wasn't much. I approached my practicing of this piece with utmost seriousness, repeating the sequence over and over on my drum, determined to get it right.

It didn't take long for my practice time to spill over to outside the music room. I began using my hands to drum my part on tabletops, on chairs, on my thighs. Every flat surface became my instrument, much to the dismay of the adults in my life.

After a while, drumming this part—or something like it—became a way for me to let off energy or to help me think while doing homework. I had other fidgety habits, but learning this part became a more explicit and more focused way for me to channel my need to move when most would rather I sit still without shaking the desk or making noise.

At times, my parents or teachers would express concern about how often I seemed physically restless. I was never taken anywhere for an examination or diagnosed with anything, but to those who most regularly observed my need always to shift or move in some way, I often seemed distracted. At times, I admit that I was, but I think that most elementary-age children are. It's just that the way I did it was perhaps more observable than others' chosen methods.

And things haven't changed much since those days. When sitting to write or while trying to think, I still feel the need to move to some unspoken or unspecified rhythm. I'll tap my pencil on my desk, or drum with my thumbs on my thighs, or bounce my leg. Even as I type this sentence, I'm moving my foot back and forth under the table, for no reason other than that it helps me focus. I completely own up to my fidgety ways, even as most of the time I'm unaware that I'm engaging in them.

When working on a project of some kind that involves sitting for an extended period of time, you may be able to relate to this need to move. If you've ever clicked a pen while writing a report at your desk, or twirled a paperclip while sitting in a meeting, or tapped your pencil or highlighter while reading homework, you know something of the same fidgety sorts of impulses that I mention in my story.

But why do we feel the need to do this? Why do we—whether

we're aware of it or not—reach for some small object to roll around in our hand while trying to pay attention to the person speaking at the front of the room or while doing something else that has required that we stay put in one spot for a while?

As mentioned in Chapter 1, handling these small items can actually help us concentrate and remain engaged in whatever other tasks we need to accomplish. When we need to stay focused on something, our brains may need more stimulation than the responsibility at hand requires of us. Listening to a presentation or reading a book may not be enough for our minds to remain fixated; they need an additional action of some kind to maintain an optimal level of interest.[1]

When we're able, we create this stimulation for ourselves by reaching for a pen to click or a stress ball to squeeze, or by drumming on the arms of our chair. We rely on the tactile action of moving and feeling a small object in our hands without needing to look at it or turn our attention to it so that we can focus on something else. We fidget so that we have that extra boost of brainpower to complete whatever primary job in front of us needs it.

Sometimes that primary job is our prayer life. And as I've mentioned, sometimes sitting still for that doesn't work for us, either. As much as anything else, trying to settle in to concentrate for a time of prayer might involve our minds wandering to our to-do lists or, in some cases, even dozing off. Is it okay to fidget while praying, or to pray while fidgeting?

FIDGETING WITH FRINGES

The use of handling objects as part of a prayer practice goes back quite a long way, including the earliest days of Moses leading the Israelites in the wilderness.

The Lord said to Moses: [38]Speak to the Israelites, and tell them to make fringes on the corners of their garments throughout their generations and to put a blue cord on the fringe at each corner. [39]You have the fringe so that, when you see it, you will remember all the commandments of the Lord and do them, and not follow the lust of your own heart and your own eyes. [40]So you shall remember and do all my commandments, and you shall be holy to your God. [41]I am the Lord your God, who brought you out of the land of Egypt, to be your God: I am the Lord your God. (Numbers 15:37-41)

First, we should mention what causes God to tell Moses to pass this command on to the Israelites. Just before this passage, the people are in the wilderness, still wandering during their 40-year pre-Promised Land settlement, and they discover that one of their own is gathering sticks. In itself, this wouldn't be a problem, except the man was doing so on the Sabbath. In other words, this man was performing an act of work on a day when he'd been explicitly commanded not to.

We don't know the man's motivations for collecting sticks on the Sabbath. Maybe he'd meant to the day prior and forgot or put it off too long. Maybe he struggled with sitting still and needed to get out and calm his nerves with a simple act of twig gathering. While we aren't clued in to his reasoning, we are told of the unfortunate consequences for his actions: such an incident was without precedent and thus did not yet have a form of reprimand or punishment in place, so God decided he was to be taken outside the camp and stoned to death.[2] That escalated quickly.

In order to avoid any future episode like this, God tells Moses to tell the Israelites to add fringes to the corners of their garments to help them to remember God's many commandments—including the one to keep the Sabbath as a day of rest from all work—and remain in the proper confines of what it means to live and remain faithful as God's people.

Later in Deuteronomy, God reiterates this command to make these fringes at the ends of one's clothing:

You shall make tassels on the four corners of the cloak with which you cover yourself. (Deuteronomy 22:12)

These tassels eventually take on their own unique name, *tzitzit*, as well as a particular way to make them. *Tzitzit* are tied into a series of knots that, given the number of strands one uses and the number of knots tied, adds up to 613 to equal the number of commandments in the Mosaic law.[3]

Tzitzit make more than one appearance in the Gospels, as it was apparent that Jesus observed this command himself. In Matthew 9:20, a hemorrhaging woman reaches for the fringes of Jesus' cloak in hopes of being healed; others in need of cures from illness make similar attempts in Mark 6:56. *Tzitzit* are still in use on Jewish prayer shawls and other articles of clothing, still serving as reminders of God's commands to live as a people with a unique identity.

Such fringes may have been useful as visual reminders. After being told to add these to their garments, they could look down, see these *tzitzit*, and remember their faith much the same as a Christian might by looking at their cross necklace. But beyond sight alone, one can rub such fringes or pendants between two fingers while anxious and in need of some small action to soothe one's nervous energy. In this way, such fringes become tactile reminders as well as visual ones, aids in prayer even if one's prayer is little more than rolling them around for reassurance that they are there; symbols of a larger presence that we may seek to remember in desperation, sadness, or celebration.

PERMISSION TO FIDGET: PRAYER BEADS

In a spirit similar to the *tzitzit*, various Christian traditions have developed a way of praying using prayer beads as a guide.

When most people think of prayer beads, the most common image that may come to mind with those familiar with the general concept might be the Catholic rosary. To be sure, this is the most popular rendering of this prayer aide, but far from the only possibility. Before we get to that, we should examine the use of prayer beads in general.

When we talk about prayer beads, we mean a series of beads strung together in a particular and intentional way, with smaller beads alternating with larger ones to form a pattern. In many of these arrangements, there may be one smaller line of beads diverging from the circle while remaining connected and featuring a crucifix or empty cross at the end. This usually serves as the point where one's time of prayer begins and ends.

The practice of using prayer beads involves running one's fingers slowly around the pattern, stopping at each bead to say the prayer associated with it. Any particular bead may serve as an invitation to say popular memorized prayers such as the Lord's Prayer, the Hail Mary, or the Jesus Prayer, or one may offer one's own petitions for people or situations for which one is concerned. The type of arrangement one uses and the Christian tradition one is most familiar with will influence the specific prayers the beads represent.

Since I think my reading audience may be more non-Catholic in nature and because bead patterns other than the rosary might be less familiar, I'm choosing to give a Protestant pattern of prayer beads as an example.

A typical arrangement of Protestant prayer beads has a large cross with 33 beads total. Next to the cross is a large bead called the "invitatory bead" which, as the name implies, serves as our invitation to this time of prayer. Aside from this invitatory bead, there are four other large beads that in the overall pattern serve as the four points of the cross; for this reason they are called "cruciform beads." In between the cruciform beads are sets of seven smaller beads, called "week beads."[4]

The possibilities for how you move around this arrangement are infinite. As an easy example, you may use the invitatory bead as a simple address to God such as "O God" or "Heavenly Father" or "Gracious Creator" or "Divine Mother" or whatever your preferred title for God is while praying. Each cruciform bead could serve as a time to say the Lord's Prayer or Jesus Prayer ("Lord Jesus, Son of God, have mercy on me, a sinner."). Each set of smaller beads could represent statements about God or Jesus from scripture, people you want to remember in prayer, or verses from the Psalms.

Different seasons of the church year might present opportunities for beads to take on other representations. During Lent a set of week beads could serve as a time to speak or remember Jesus' seven statements from the cross. During Eastertide, the four cruciform beads could be moments to prayerfully proclaim, "Christ is risen!" Advent could inspire use of beads as traditional proclamations from Isaiah associated with Jesus, or during Christmas the cruciform beads could be a time to sing a verse of "Silent Night." While prayer beads provide a structure for prayer, they also invite creativity.

As an example, here is one of many patterns of prayer that could be used with Protestant prayer beads.

Cross: In the name of God the Creator, Redeemer, and Sustainer, amen.

Invitatory Bead: O God, guide me during this time of prayer.

1st Cruciform Bead: The Jesus prayer

1st Set of Week Beads: Remember 7 ways God has been with you this past week.

2nd Cruciform Bead: The Jesus prayer

2nd Set of Week Beads: Offer up 7 concerns you have for yourself or others.

3rd Cruciform Bead: The Jesus prayer

3rd Set of Week Beads: Remember 7 people going through a hard time.

4th Cruciform Bead: The Jesus prayer

4th Set of Week Beads: Think of 7 ways you may need guidance or help this coming week.

Invitatory Bead: O Spirit, thank you for your presence.

Cross: In the name of God the Creator, Redeemer, and Sustainer, amen.

Prayer beads serve several purposes at once. First, they provide a guide for people unsure of what to pray about during any particular time set aside to do so. If you come to such a time with a list at hand like the above regarding what each bead represents, you can move around the beads, knowing what to pray as you stop at each one.

Second, prayer beads also serve as a natural fidget object to keep our minds engaged as we pray. Handling the beads, rolling them around between our fingers as we offer our joys, concerns, and petitions to God, helps us focus on our chosen spiritual practice. We may be less likely to start thinking about our grocery list or to nod off because we have something to occupy the part of our brain that would be tempted to steer us in that direction.

We don't necessarily need prayer beads to engage in fidgety prayer, but we can borrow the concepts they use for other objects. Both the *tzitzit* and prayer beads show us that fidgeting while praying is allowed, and may even be beneficial to remaining engaged with the practice.

NO, REALLY, GO AHEAD AND FIDGET

In case you had not yet picked up on it, you have permission to fidget while praying. In fact, doing so will probably help you focus on your prayer more than trying to will yourself to sit completely still. That's not to say that some people can't do that—indeed, many can and do. But not all of us are wired to be able to still our bodies and focus our minds to the point where we're able to remain focused throughout the exercise without becoming distracted, bored, or sleepy.

This is okay. This is normal. And while you could attempt methods to get past encountering those issues in your prayer life in order to be still and know that God is God in the most literal sense, using mind engagement aides such as prayer beads, a rubber ball, a pen, a small cross, or something else is just as valuable and valid a method as those suggested to keep working through your fidgety tendencies.

Sitting lotus position in perfect silence is not the only mark of a true prayer master. There is no right or wrong way to pray. There are ways more effective than others, and that varies from person to person. You aren't doing it wrong if you need something to fiddle with. And if you've gone your whole life thinking or being taught otherwise, here finally is your invitation to leave such thoughts behind, and to find something more authentic to what you need in order to connect to God.

PRAYER PRACTICE AND QUESTIONS FOR REFLECTION

1. Think of an object that you tend to fidget with while working on other projects. It might be an office item or something that represents your faith. Maybe you already use a rosary or another form of prayer beads. If it's often the same item, have you ever thought about why that is? If your object is faith-related or some-

thing more significant than a paper clip or pencil, is there a story behind it, such as where you got it or who gave it to you?

2. Sit down with your chosen object and examine how it could be used for prayer similar to a strand of prayer beads. Similar to how one is meant to move one's fingers from one bead to another, think of how you could use your item in that way. For instance, if you have a pen, you could move to a new part of your prayer with each click. With a smooth, flat stone, you could begin a new part every time you flip it over in your hand. Imagine the possibilities that will be unique to your own object.

3. Choose a number of specific little prayers you will say. Beginning with a basic address to God and ending with a similar gesture of thankfulness or closing, decide how many petitions or times for reflection you will use in between. As a way to start, you could use the Biblically significant number of seven, making the fourth a common prayer such as the Lord's Prayer.

4. After completing your series of prayers, reflect on how and whether using an object was helpful. What could you change in the future, whether adding more prayers or structuring it differently, with more petitions or times to offer common memorized prayers.

NOTES

[1] Katherine Isbister. "Fidget toys aren't just hype," *The Conversation*, online, accessed September 21, 2017.

[2] Thomas Dozeman. "The Book of Numbers," from *The New Interpreters Bible* (Nashville: Abingdon, 1998), 128.

[3] Kristen Vincent. *A Bead and a Prayer*. (Nashville: Upper Room, 2013), 30.

[4] *Ibid.*, 18-19.

7

WHILE TRAVELING

*O*f the many vacations my family of origin took over the years, one that we took in the summer of 2000 ranks among the most infamous. Even to this day, the four of us—my father, mother, brother, and myself—refer to it only as "the trip to Maine." But just those four words cause a slew of memories to bubble back up, and usually they're accompanied by an audible groan.

"The trip to Maine" was a two-week long drive through several New England states where, as the name suggests, our eventual destination was Maine. My grandparents used to make this annual trip themselves, but as their years advanced, they needed other family members to drive them around so they could catch up with old friends around the state.

Time and distance have softened my own view of this trip. My memories of that region's beautiful landscapes, shimmering coasts, charming small towns, and delicious food have overtaken the parts of that trip that I'd rather forget, which largely consist of being stuck in a minivan for hours at a time with all of us growing more irritable by the minute. There were stretches of that drive where we just weren't happy to be near each other in such a small space for so long. We could choose to remember other parts of that trip instead, but that aspect of our experience especially stands out to us, even so many years later.

I do have at least one positive memory of the car ride portion of this trip. It was a Sunday morning, which is easy for me to remember due to what happened. The six of us were settling in for another lengthy drive; I myself had just popped on my headphones to listen to some music. Before I could allow my chosen tunes to carry my mind away from my immediate confines, however, I caught a snippet of my grandparents lamenting that we had to be on the road rather than sitting in a church service. Having both been longtime stalwarts of their small congregation in New Jersey, they were missing being a part of a time of worship that morning.

Their solution to this problem was to begin singing some of their favorite hymns while we cruised along at 65 miles an hour. The one I most clearly remember is "Amazing Grace," but they sang several that day. My parents may have joined in at some points, but I was content to listen, postponing my own music so I could hear them. If we were going to be stuck in this car for so long, especially during such a sacred hour for many Christian believers, they were going to do their best to make it holy, if only for a few minutes.

We travel for many different reasons. The obvious reason for all travel is to get from one place to another, but the reasons we need or want to get there vary. We may face a daily commute to work, whether a few minutes' drive down the road or a longer timeframe of up to an hour either in our own car or on public transportation. We travel because we need to get our families to school or to extracurricular activities. We travel to appointments or when we're heading out for the evening to a ballgame, concert, or dinner.

And then there are the special vacation trips to new or familiar places. This may be a once-in-a-lifetime tour of another country or continent, or a state or region that has always been on your dream list of places to visit. Or you may have a spot that you daydream about all year long and that brings you relief once you finally get back to it. Whether a familiar beach, campground, city, or cabin, it is a place that has become a respite from your everyday responsibilities.

That's one of the key features of most road trips: they're different from what you know. They feature time away from work, from home, and from their accompanying routines and obligations. They bring experiences that are new and at least partially unknown even if you've been coming to the same place every year. Maybe you have an idea of where you want to go and what you look forward to doing once you get there, but there is still a novelty and uncertainty about what might happen once you arrive. Still, that newness is the point.

But there also come those times of travel that carry less excitement or anticipation. Our work commutes or ritualistic drives to the soccer fields might not be all that inspiring. This could be due to the sheer length of the trip; up to an hour or two lost every day just driving or sitting on a train, and perhaps not always with the most considerate or boundary-respecting companions. The trips to another practice or another meeting might bring resentment about what you could be doing instead if only you could remain at home. Likewise, some vacations end up being "trips to Maine," where everyone is irritable or plans don't work out the way we thought they would.

Can our times of travel be redeemed? Is there a way to approach these times in a way that brings renewal or a chance to experience or acknowledge God's presence, even and especially when they're least enjoyable?

SEEING THE MANNA

Now when the people complained in the hearing of the Lord about their misfortunes, the Lord heard it and his anger was kindled. Then the fire of the Lord burned against them, and consumed some outlying parts of the camp. ²But the people cried out to Moses; and Moses prayed to the Lord, and the fire abated. ³So that place was called Taberah, because the fire of the Lord burned against them.

⁴The rabble among them had a strong craving; and the Israelites also wept again, and said, "If only we had meat to eat! ⁵We remember the fish we used to eat in Egypt for nothing, the cucumbers, the melons, the leeks, the onions, and the garlic; ⁶but now our strength is dried up, and there is nothing at all but this manna to look at." ⁷Now the manna was like coriander seed, and its color was like the color of gum resin. ⁸The people went around and gathered it, ground it in mills or beat it in mortars, then boiled it in pots and made cakes of it; and the taste of it was like the taste of cakes baked with oil. ⁹When the dew fell on the camp in the night, the manna would fall with it. (Numbers 11:1-9)

Whereas my family had "the trip to Maine," the Israelites in the first few books of the Hebrew scriptures had "the trip to the Promised Land." This trip was much longer than two weeks (forty years) and featured conflicts and hardships that were more serious than being stuck in a minivan with one's family, although I imagine that having to be around the same people for so long became a cause for irritation and grumbling every so often.

The main issue in this story, however, is the food rather than the company. After an unfortunate episode where the people's complaining gets God angry enough that Moses has to intervene on the people's behalf (something he has to do more than once), we hear one cause for the people being upset: they're tired of eating manna. They want a little more variety in their road trip diet, and specifically, they want to eat meat.

Manna was first introduced in the story back in Exodus 16, where again the Israelites are grumbling about wanting something to eat. In response, God gives instructions that every day with the morning dew, this white flaky substance will appear for them to gather and bake into breads or cakes. Exodus describes its taste as sweet, "like wafers made with honey" (Exodus 16:31).

The word "manna" itself means "What is it?" This is the question that the Israelites ask when they first see it. Moses' response is "it is the bread that the LORD has given you to eat" (Exodus 16:15). This gift of manna in response to the people's crying out for something to eat is the Israelites' experience of the wilderness in a nutshell: they crave sustenance and relief, God provides heavenly gifts, and Moses points out these gifts and explains or interprets or gives instructions regarding what they are.

Back to this episode in Numbers. The people have been eating manna for quite a while now and are getting restless. They want meat to eat, and as they have done before, are starting to reminisce about how great the food was back when they were suffering oppression under the Egyptians' thumb. They've taken to rationalizing that their former lives of slavery are preferable to what they have now, because at least they got to enjoy a variety of food.

The trip is getting long, the people are becoming tired of their companions and their leadership, and they want something else to eat. They've begun missing the gifts of God all around them on this journey, and Moses is finding it more difficult to point them out to them. And yet these gifts from heaven still appear every morning to be seen and gathered and consumed and enjoyed. But other aspects of the trip are causing the people to miss them more and more.

JEFFREY A. NELSON

REFRAMING OUR JOURNEYS

Most religious traditions have a spiritual practice where believers may make pilgrimages to places of significance to their faith. For Islam, traveling to Mecca (the Hajj) is one of the five pillars central to its observance. Jews may visit the Western Wall of the destroyed Temple and leave written prayers between its massive bricks. Many Christians make trips to spots around Jerusalem, Galilee, and Bethlehem to visit sites associated with Jesus' life.

The concept of pilgrimage is rooted in the idea that one is transformed through travel; that we learn more about ourselves and grow in our relationship with God by journeying to these places. Pilgrimage is a tangible act by which we physically move ourselves in order to seek spiritual movement. In actions such as walking, seeing these places with our own eyes, touching them as allowed, feeling and breathing the air and atmosphere of these special places, we gain a greater understanding of what they mean that reading or hearing about them from afar cannot accomplish.

A better-known pilgrimage for the Christian faith is the Camino de Santiago in Spain, which is a walk of anywhere between 200 and 800 kilometers (depending on the route) to the Cathedral of Santiago de Compostela, where the remains of St. James the Great are kept. Hundreds of pilgrims travel various roads and paths to visit this site every year. As with every pilgrimage, the walking itself is part of the experience: one passes through many villages and is privy to endless countryside landscapes along the way, which immerses the pilgrim in the geography and culture of this sacred place for days and weeks prior to their reaching their destination.

In an address in the cathedral, Pope Benedict XVI made this observation about the purpose of pilgrimage:

> To go on pilgrimage is not simply to visit a place to admire its
> treasures of nature, art or history. To go on pilgrimage really

means to step out of ourselves in order to encounter God where he has revealed himself, where his grace has shone with particular splendor and produced rich fruits of conversion and holiness among those who believe.[1]

As with many vacations we take, to go on a pilgrimage is to leave what we know behind in order to become a part of something wholly different for a time. It may deepen our appreciation for our home life, but it does so by showing us something about God, ourselves, and the world that we hadn't previously experienced and wouldn't have known without going. And the meaning is in the traveling itself as much as in the arrival.

What does this have to do with our daily commute to work or to the kids' dance rehearsal? How could we use the principles of pilgrimage and apply them to the travel that we know almost every day? Are we really meant to believe that these regular trips are in any way comparable to visiting holy places in Israel or Spain?

Pilgrimage reveals to travelers how God is present not just in sites set aside for divine encounters and personal reverence, but also in our everyday lives. To travel to these places is also to realize that God is where we usually find ourselves, because this sacred experience opens us to such an understanding. Every journey takes on something of its character, just as other spiritual practices show us similar truths.

When we drive to our job, or to our children's activities, or to our own evenings out, we are meant to remember that God is with us in the traveling and will be present in the arrival. We may take some of these trips begrudgingly, wishing like the Israelites that something about them could be different or that we could be back home. But there is manna all around us whether we can see it or not. God's gifts surround us as we travel, including when we would rather not, although we may not always be ready to see or receive them.

There is manna in the conversation we may have with our son or daughter on the way to the ball field. There is manna among the other parents gathered to watch practice or swap stories as they wait. There is manna in the other people with whom we share a train into the office. There is manna in a Friday night spent with a spouse, partner, or group at the pub, theater, club, or restaurant. There is manna by the lake, in the surf of the ocean, at the amusement park, at the hotel, or in the woods.

Every summer, my family spends a week at a condo overlooking the Atlantic Ocean in Florida. The drive from our house takes 14 hours, and depending on how motivated we are, we may try to make the entire trip in one day or break it up by stopping midway for the night. With two children accompanying us, we may want to get the drive out of the way as quick as we can while knowing we'll need to stop every so often for bathroom breaks. Keeping them entertained and well-fed with snacks adds an extra dimension to the challenge, as each hour seems to get longer than the last.

This journey seems easier in some years than in others, for a variety of reasons. I have found one trick to keep in mind as we go—one visual to hold in my active thought as we drive along—that helps me remember why we are yet again putting ourselves through this long trip.

I remember that the following morning, I will rise before everyone else, when the sun's light is just beginning to illuminate the sky and the waters. I will pour a cup of coffee and sneak over to the door of our condo's balcony, where I will slip out and lean my arms on the railing.

Here I will catch my first glimpse of the vast ocean that the night made too dark to see the previous day, putting a picture to the crashing against the sand. I will take a deep breath of the salty air and listen to the gulls and pelicans as they soar overhead. I will take in the immense beauty of creation while appreciating everything that I don't understand about it, and I will give thanks that I can once again call this place home for a week. And I will open myself to the God who brought such grandeur into being. I will be far from a church sanctuary, but will know the divine in this sacred place anyway.

Knowing that this will be my experience the following morning, I may see in the meantime the ways the imminent presence of the divine is with us as we roll down the miles of highway standing between us and where we want to be.

God's gifts may be found during our vacations, our mundane trips to the office or the store, our weekend outings. When we are able to recognize this, we may build our own internal shrines to remember, and perhaps even be moved to sing "Amazing Grace" as we ride along.

PRAYER PRACTICE AND QUESTIONS FOR REFLECTION

1. Where will you be required to travel in the coming week, either for work, family, or fun? Choose one trip, and identify the following: those you'll be traveling with, why you'll need to travel, who you might see once you arrive, and what you might be able to expect to happen once you get there.

2. Before starting your journey, ask God to open you to God's presence. Prepare yourself to receive the manna that you may be able to see along the way, in experiences both positive and negative.

3. As you begin your trip, ask yourself how God is with each person you see or interact with. How are they behaving; what might they need? For example, is there someone who seems stressed or sad or bored or lonely? Say a quick prayer for each of them, trusting that God knows what they are seeking.

4. Once you arrive, notice the sights, sounds, and mood around you. Pay attention to the conversations and interactions that you see and hear. Is there excitement, or joy, or routine, or anxiety, or a hushed tone? What is happening to cause this?

How is God in the midst of it, or how might you wish God to be?

5. Notice your own reactions to all of this. Certain things might cause you to feel happy, or upset, or nervous, or relieved. Why might any of these be the case?

6. When you complete your journey back home, think back to where you were. With time and distance, are you able to consider any of it differently? Are you able to see better why someone might have made a certain statement, or why someone might have seemed to be feeling a certain way? Consider why you might have reacted to certain points of the experience in particular ways.

7. Conclude by thanking God for the day and for the journey you just made.

NOTES

[1] Pope Benedict XVI. "Address of the Holy Father Benedict XVI," November 6, 2010, online, accessed October 7, 2017.

8
WHILE WALKING

I used to live near a state park that featured a pond for fishing, pavilions for picnics, and trails for walking. Whenever I wanted to get away for an hour or more, I just needed to take a few minutes' drive over to this park where I'd pocket my keys, choose a path, and head into the woods.

The trails in this park were as picturesque as anywhere else. At some points they wound through the trees, their canopy providing shade as the birds tweeted their songs and the squirrels jumped from branch to branch. At others they opened into spacious meadows where the path cut through tall grass and fields of wheat. Some parts ran parallel to brooks and streams, and every so often a small bridge would connect one side to the other.

I admit that I wasn't always good at paying attention on my walks. Sometimes I walked just to get some form of exercise before returning to a desk covered in work. It was the principle of maybe getting a little out of breath that motivated me more than appreciating the scenery along the way. At other times, however, I'd be able to notice some curiosities along the way.

One such memorable instance came as I passed a group of aspen trees close to the trailside, the bark of which were covered in carvings. These consisted mostly of names or initials inside hearts. I slowed to get a better view of past hikers' botanical graffiti and happened to look up where I saw one message that seemed to stand out among the others: "Luv my frog."

This particular carving caught my fascination for several reasons. First, the words themselves. A plain reading indicated that somebody loved their frog. But who or what was the frog? Did it indicate an actual frog, was this a pet name for a person, or was it something else entirely? Second, this carving was set up at an impressive height: someone had to climb eight or ten feet up the side of the tree in order to broadcast their amorous feelings to subsequent passers-by. They had gone through a lot of effort to leave their mark on this tree, to immortalize their "luv" for their frog.

The truth resides with the person who ascended with their pocketknife at some prior time. The story of who loves their frog and who wanted every park visitor to know it for all time, may never be told beyond those who witnessed it happen, as well as anyone who would slow their walk long enough to notice.

As it happened, I was one such fortunate slow walker. If I hadn't decided to be deliberate about my walk that day, to hike at a leisurely pace that would allow me to notice things like someone's "luv my frog" etching, I would have missed this declaration of amphibious affection, and probably a lot of other things as well.

When was the last time you took a walk? While not on the same scale as being able to head to a retreat center for a day, taking even 20 minutes to walk can seem like a privilege that an increasing amount of people don't have. We may rationalize this with the usual litany of defenses: work hours are too long, the family has too many obligations on evenings and weekends, the end of the day brings a desire for rest rather than more activity.

The very thought of setting aside a half hour for walking might cause stressful thoughts, just as much as setting aside that time for prayer. This has the exact opposite effect that such activities are meant to cause. Walking can be a low-impact form of exercise, but it can also be a way to wind down or break up a day's worth of demands. It can be a chance to set down those responsibilities for a while and, as in my "luv my frog" hike, notice things you wouldn't otherwise have been able to see were it not for making it a point to look up and look out from your to-do list.

On any given day in my neighborhood, I see a wide variety of walkers. We live in a low-traffic area, and many of my fellow residents love taking advantage as often as they can. Retirees pass one another an hour or two after sunrise, exchanging pleasantries as they go. After the workday has ended, parents push kids in strollers and friends engage in casual conversation as their leashed dogs trot in front of them. After getting off the bus, school-age kids move between houses to visit or to take the shortcut through backyards down to the ice cream stand.

If my area is any indication, many people still value walking not just as a way to be active but also to be social or just to be outside for a while. Of course, there are indoor options as well: places like the YMCA have indoor tracks for walking, and some companies have marked "walking paths" that wind through their hallways as encouragement for employees to be active for a while in the midst of the workday. Rather than meet with parishioners in their office, some of my pastoral colleagues schedule "walking meetings" as a way to move while they work.

These sorts of examples highlight several things about walking. First, it shows that many still value it as a way to get the body moving. They may have too many constraints that prevent gym access, but a short jaunt through their neighborhood or workplace is important enough that they'll make time to do it. Second, it shows creativity in how walking can be built into one's day, whether it involves identifying possible fellow walkers, using walking as a way to do two things at once, such as doing it while meeting with clients or as a way to get the baby to go to sleep. As with any practice—spiritual or not—a strong enough desire to commit to something might involve thinking outside the box in order to do it.

LISTENING FOR GOD'S VOICE WHILE WALKING

Now that we've thought about the physical value of walking, we should spend time thinking about its spiritual value. When beginning to incorporate walking into one's day, we might not always think of its spiritual possibilities, nor might we set out to use it as a form of prayer. In fact, most people who decide they want to start walking a few times a week or every day usually do so for reasons other than as a practice for seeking God's presence. But as with the other activities discussed in this book, there are ways to incorporate prayer into one's walking, just as one might combine it with other activities like the examples given earlier.

First, let's reflect for a moment on a prominent Biblical figure who didn't intend a walk to yield a spiritual outcome:

> Meanwhile Saul, still breathing threats and murder against the disciples of the Lord, went to the high priest ²and asked him for letters to the synagogues at Damascus, so that if he found any who belonged to the Way, men or women, he might bring them bound to Jerusalem. ³Now as he was going along and approaching Damascus, suddenly a light from heaven flashed around him. ⁴He fell to the ground and heard a voice saying to him, "Saul, Saul, why do you persecute me?" ⁵He asked, "Who are you, Lord?" The reply came, "I am Jesus, whom you are persecuting. ⁶But get up and enter the city, and you will be told what you are to do." ⁷The men who were traveling with him stood speechless because they heard the voice but saw no one. ⁸Saul got up from the ground, and though his eyes were open, he could see nothing; so they led him by the hand and brought him into Damascus. ⁹For three days he was without sight, and neither ate nor drank. (Acts 9:1-9)

Before we delve into this scriptural story, I should add the disclaimer up front that not every time of walking prayer will be this dramatic. However, it provides a few insights as to how walking may open us to God's presence.

First, we see that Saul was not in the best internal state when we meet him in Acts. We actually read the first mention of him a few verses earlier as he is overseeing and approving the stoning of Stephen, who is usually deemed the first Christian martyr. And now Saul is on his way to Damascus to, if not do more of the same, at least arrest those who identify themselves with the blossoming Jesus Movement.

On the way to complete his mission, however, Saul is knocked over by a (literally) blinding light as a divine voice questions his motives. For his own part, he seems to recognize the one speaking even as he asks who is doing so, because he addresses the disembodied interrupter as "Lord." The voice answers that it is, in fact, Jesus, who wants to know why Saul is treating his followers with such vitriol and violence. Having identified himself, he instructs Saul to complete his journey, but his purpose has now shifted significantly.

Again, not many walks will feature blinding lights and audible instructions from Jesus. Nevertheless, we can take several general principles from this passage to help us think about walking as a spiritual practice.

First, we can expect to be surprised. Prayer is not a magical exercise that yields incredible life-changing insights or results every time we do it, but making it a regular observance can create space within us to be surprised when such times occur.

Second, as with the story of the transfiguration in an earlier chapter, we see the importance of listening. Given how this encounter presents itself, Saul has little choice in the matter, but he stops to listen to Jesus. This comes after he recognizes who is speaking to him. Any form of prayer, including while walking, brings with it a need to open oneself to what God wants to say to us.

Finally, this story shows a reliance on others. Saul is blinded by his experience for a few days and has to rely first on his walking companions and eventually on a wise and faithful man named Ananias for guidance, both to find where he needs to go and to interpret what this confrontation by Jesus means for his life. Sometimes walking with others may be more appealing than walking alone, and we may need the assistance of spiritually insightful people to help us understand what may come up during our walking: what we thought or prayed about, or what revelations and realizations came to us as we did so.

LEARNING FROM THE LABYRINTH

In Chapter 1, I told the story of an experience while walking a labyrinth. The design of a labyrinth is older than its associations with prayer, but its combination of movement and spiritual reflection have made it a popular practice in recent centuries.

With its typical design being a series of twists and turns around one another, a labyrinth is sometimes mistaken for being a maze. Rather, a labyrinth is a single path with one entrance and one exit, which are one and the same. Labyrinths are usually arranged in a circular pattern with the center designated as a place to stop, rest, pray, or reflect. Because of the way the path bends around itself in this traditional design, each layer of the path between the edge and the center is called a "circuit." The number of circuits helps the walker know how large and how long the labyrinth is.

There are two common numbers of circuits in a labyrinth. The "classical" design has seven circuits and dates back to ancient Greece. The other most well-known design is the 11-circuit labyrinth often called "Chartres-style," named after the Chartres Cathedral in France which helped popularize it. The center of the

Chartres labyrinth, often consisting of six partial circles resembling the petals of a flower, is sometimes called the "rosette."[1]

Today's labyrinth practice embodies the idea of being on a journey, a time of spiritual reflection where the walking itself is an act of prayer. As you walk toward the center, you are journeying with God as your guide. As mentioned earlier with the story of Saul, you may or may not experience a grand revelation every time you walk a labyrinth; the meaning is in the walking. Lauren Artress explains:

> Walking the labyrinth does not demand a great amount of concentration in order to benefit from the experience. The sheer act of walking a complicated path—which discharges energy—begins to focus on the mind. A quiet mind does not happen automatically. But the labyrinth experience sensitizes us, educates us, and helps us distinguish superficial extraneous thoughts from the "thought" that comes from our soul level and that each of us longs to hear. Many of us are discovering that this is much easier to do when our whole body is moving—when we are walking.[2]

In other words, the key to the labyrinth—or any form of prayerful activity—is the action of walking itself. When one is deliberate about opening oneself to each step on the path while letting go of worries such as whether something grand will happen or how much longer one has until reaching the center, the greater chance the experience will do what it is really meant to do.

The primary goals of the labyrinth, as explained by Artress, are several. First, there is the energy used to walk. Recall that in my labyrinth story, I needed to burn nervous energy and was not going to benefit from trying to use a devotional book while sitting still. Have you or someone you know ever said, "I need to get out of here and walk for a while?" The labyrinth is a perfect activity for moments like that.

Second, like most other spiritual practices, repeated and regular use of the labyrinth helps condition people to receive what it offers. Observing a prayer practice just once or in an intermittent way will not be enough to cultivate the openness to God's presence that it is meant to provide.

Finally, over time, the openness that walking a labyrinth helps create will help us notice the small things that may be key to the concerns or wonders that we've brought to our time of prayer. We'll be able to notice the little "luv my frog" sorts of messages that God may be sharing with us. We'll be able to quiet the noise inside us and discern God's voice underneath it.

For most of us, a labyrinth is not readily available. But we have access to indoor or outdoor tracks, the streets of our own neighborhood, the trails of state or local parks, and other places most ideal for walking. Even without the circuits of this special pattern, we may nevertheless apply the labyrinth's principles and lessons to our own times of walking, wherever is most convenient for us to do it.

Whether walking is already a part of your day or you've long thought about adding it as a way to be more active or to unwind, it can also be a natural opportunity to commune with God just by noticing what is around you and within you. By bringing an attitude of openness to your walking, you may be able to hear God's voice speaking to your heart and see the subtle messages placed along your path waiting to be discovered.

PRAYER PRACTICE AND QUESTIONS FOR REFLECTION

1. Identify a place and time for walking. Take proper account of safety issues and other possible concerns, e.g., whether the traffic on the streets closest to your house may be too heavy. Is this feasible for you to do first thing in the morning, on your lunch break from work, or after getting home? Be realistic about the variables involved.

2. Say a small prayer before beginning. Do you have a question or issue you've been struggling with related to some aspect of your life? Offer it to God. Sometimes even whispering or speaking it out loud may help center you for the walking ahead. Entrust these thoughts or questions to God, letting them go instead of trying to concentrate on them during your walk.

3. Begin walking. Notice the speed of your pace; don't try to hurry to your destination or to complete your route. Slowing your steps will help your thoughts and senses do the same.

4. Be deliberate about looking around, rather than just at the road or trail. Take time to see and hear what is around you, to note things like the weather, other people, the sights, sounds, and activities of nature such as the plants or birds. If you've walked this route before, what might you notice that you've never seen before, even though it's always been there?

5. Notice what you are thinking and feeling as you walk. What reactions do the sights and sounds of your surroundings cause inside you? Do they bring joy, or remind you of something or someone, or spark your curiosity? Prayerfully consider how or why these emotions, memories, and reflections may have come to you. Hold them until they become distracting, then let them go.

When you reach the end of your walk, say another prayer of gratitude for the gifts it may have brought through sensory experiences or through thoughts or feelings you may want to spend more time with. Who could you further process these things with later? Write some notes to yourself or journal if you think it will help you remember.

NOTES

[1] Lauren Artress. *Walking a Sacred Path*. (New York: Riverhead, 2006), 58.

[2] Ibid., 71.

9

WHILE CREATING ART

I walked into the shop, a garage-sized structure behind a house which itself was hidden away from the road. A homemade sign out by the mailbox served as the only indicator that this place was here, though judging from what I saw and what the owner told me, it wasn't lacking for business.

I met her a few weeks prior at an outdoor arts festival. Her booth joined a bevy of others along the winding sidewalks of a public park with a manmade lake in the center, joining people selling custom jewelry, wine bottles made into oil lamps, acrylic paintings, homemade confections, and hand-stitched clothing such as scarves and wraps.

By trade she was a sculptor and a potter. Her work drew me over because I, then just a few years into my time at an area church, had been on the hunt for a clay communion set; a chalice and plate on which to set the elements whenever I would preside during morning worship. For me, there is something special about a homespun set over one forged from metal. I find an authenticity to it that I appreciate and that I wanted to feature during that important sacramental moment.

After browsing what she had on hand and not finding

anything that fit what I was after, I asked if she'd ever been asked to make something for such a purpose. Her eyes lit up as she expressed great interest in this possible project, and we arranged to meet at her shop after she tried her hand at making it.

And there we were, surrounded by much of her work: mugs, statuettes, vases, dishes, bowls, candle holders, all with price tags hanging from strings or with small stickers in prominent places on each item. She brought me toward the rear of her workspace where a plate and chalice sat, a matching set newly made.

At this point, she shared a little of what went into the creative process for her. She shared that she was a Christian and a member of another area church herself—as it happened, one that used to share a pastor with mine—and how special she'd found this particular project. Pottery is by nature slow and deliberate, and she recounted to me how she prayed as she spun her wheel, her hands carefully working their way around each piece. She prayed for their use, for my church, for me, and envisioned these petitions becoming a part of these items, fusing with and enriching the clay as she went.

What do you create? Even if you aren't a professional or an expert, what do you enjoy making with your own knowledge and skills? Do you love singing or playing an instrument, or painting, or drawing, or acting, or sewing, or crocheting, or writing? Do you love tinkering with machines or building things with wood? Do you enjoy fixing what's broken or improving things that need an upgrade, such as houses or landscaping? Do you have a green thumb, finding personal enrichment in keeping a garden or closely monitoring your trees and bushes?

Again, you don't have to be the best at any of these to enjoy them and to derive fulfillment from them. Such creative outlets satisfy something in us, offering a sense of achievement and contribution to the world in a way other than tending to our work or families. The opportunity to be creative through art or woodworking or horticulture helps us maintain our vitality in these other important areas of our lives.

These activities are also expressions of God's creativity that resides within us. As with the woman who made my pottery set, they provide yet another opportunity for prayerful reflection.

CREATED TO CREATE

At the core of who we are lies what God has placed in us when we were created. As God has made each of us unique, with accompanying gifts, so too has God given us a creative spark common to every person. It is a purpose that grounds us all as beloved beings given the gift of life. To help us consider what it is, we'll briefly explore two statements from Christian tradition.

Near the beginning of his Spiritual Exercises, Ignatius of Loyola presents a statement called the Principle and Foundation, which serves as the theological root for the entire Exercises. The first part of this statement reads as follows:

> The human person is created to praise, reverence and serve God our Lord, and by so doing save his or her soul; and it is for the human person that the other things on the face of the earth are created, as helps to the pursuit of this end.[1]

Ignatius says that our common calling as God's creatures is to "praise, reverence and serve God our Lord." What does he mean by this? How should we read this phrase, let alone the entire paragraph? Some may hear this as an obligation to participate in a never-ending worship service, which may sound incredibly unappealing. Hopefully there's another option for interpreting this.

Each of us exist as individuals, where our own personality, interests, ideas, observations, and participation in the world will never happen again after we pass on. When God made us, God did so out of creativity and love, both of which continue to reside within us every moment that follows our taking our first breath. Any time that we act upon our own desire to create, or our own feelings of love for others, we are reflecting what God first showed to us when we came into being.[2]

Praising, reverencing, and serving God happens every time we show this creativity and love. Any time an artist paints, any time a writer writes, any time a chef cooks, any time a parent nurtures a child, any time a scientist engages in analysis, any time a gardener tends vegetables or flowers, is a time when humanity is praising and serving God by doing what God did first with us. God placed within us a creative love, and whenever we act on it, we are doing what God formed us to do.

The writer of Psalm 30 puts this a different way:

I will extol you, O Lord, for you have drawn me up, and did not let my foes rejoice over me.

[2]O Lord my God, I cried to you for help, and you have healed me.

[3]O Lord, you brought up my soul from Sheol, restored me to life from among those gone down to the Pit.

[4]Sing praises to the Lord, O you his faithful ones, and give thanks to his holy name.

[5]For his anger is but for a moment; his favor is for a lifetime. Weeping may linger for the night, but joy comes with the morning.

[6]As for me, I said in my prosperity, "I shall never be moved."

[7]By your favor, O Lord, you had established me as a strong mountain; you hid your face; I was dismayed.

[8]To you, O Lord, I cried, and to the Lord I made supplication:

[9]"What profit is there in my death, if I go down to the Pit? Will the dust praise you? Will it tell of your faithfulness?

[10]Hear, O Lord, and be gracious to me! O Lord, be my helper!"

[11]You have turned my mourning into dancing; you have taken off my sackcloth and clothed me with joy,

[12]so that my soul may praise you and not be silent. O Lord my God, I will give thanks to you forever. (Psalm 30)

This Psalm begins with a personal tale of deliverance; a time of healing or restoration that the writer has experienced and through which he or she has felt God's presence. What began as a moment of suffering and of deep uncertainty has become cause for celebration, because God has brought peace, wholeness, and well-being to the writer. As observed in verse 5, "weeping may linger for the night, but joy comes with the morning." Sadness has been transformed to joy.

As a result, the psalmist praises and gives thanks to God, and invites others to do the same. He revisits his testimony that all was well for a time, but then after life took a turn it felt as if God had hidden God's face. And so he cried out, asking, "Who will praise you if I can't? Will the dust do it? Who am I if I can't praise you, or share your faithfulness with others?"

The psalmist is expressing a similar sentiment as Ignatius of Loyola in his Principle and Foundation, but with a twist. He would likely agree with Ignatius in that he has been created to praise God, and this experience of renewal has only strengthened that resolve.

Psalm 30 differs in that the writer says that he is compelled to offer God praise in all things. If he's not around to do it, who will? Maybe inanimate objects such as the dust of the ground will do it, but not really. In other words, the psalmist feels no other choice but to offer God praise with his entire self. It is part of his very being, and if he can't do it then he doesn't know who he is.

Have you ever felt an all-encompassing desire or need to create something? Have you ever experienced a moment where if you couldn't make music, or bake, or craft something with your hands, or reach out to help someone, that something inside you would explode? Have you ever been in tune with an impulse at the center of your soul that says you need to do something because it's the right and good thing to do and you are sure that it's you who must do it, because you are gifted at it and because you can?

This is the creative love God has placed in you. It is the same urgent need that the psalmist has to offer God praise, because that is what we end up doing as we share our passions and gifts, whether with others or just to enjoy them for our own leisure and replenishment. This is what Ignatius means by our purpose to praise, reverence, and glorify God in all things. Whenever we act out of the same love with which we were made, we fulfill a purpose and live into the divine center within us.

Once we discover and embrace this creative love that is within us, we begin to recognize that we have an identity and purpose rooted in God. We may learn this through our families and friends, or through our religious tradition or the culture in which we have been raised. Sometimes we may need to unlearn some things first before we can embrace or understand this about ourselves. But no matter the particulars of our first birth, or of our roles today in family, work, and life, we are foremost wonderfully made by a creative, loving God who calls each of us by name.

And when we act on that creativity placed in us, we are fulfilling what God started when we were made. To engage in our favorite creative outlets while holding this realization in the forefront of our minds can be and is a prayerful act.

CREATIVITY AS PRAYER

In his book *The Music Lesson*, accomplished bassist Victor Wooten explains his approach to music in a series of imagined conversations with a mysterious man named Michael. Michael is a mystical figure who guides Wooten to look at the spirit of musical concepts like technique, tone, dynamics, and notes, beyond the nuts and bolts of how to apply them to practicing and playing.

In one chapter, the discussion turns to the subject of how emotion can be an integral part of playing. Michael tries to get

Wooten to understand that following emotion rather than resisting it, infusing music with emotion rather than ignoring it, can deepen both the player and hearer's experience:

> "It is like trusting the river current to take you where you want to go. To fight the current could be disastrous. In each situation, whether it be in Music or in Life, take a moment to close your eyes and feel the current of your heart taking you where you need to be. After your awareness develops, you will no longer need to close your eyes. You will feel the pull of your heart's current and ride it with open eyes, allowing you to view all the astounding scenery around you. I tell you this: If you can follow the current at all times, you will not have a thing to worry about, ever."[3]

Via Michael, Wooten shows the reader that how one feels has an inevitable influence on how one plays. In the paragraph above, he advocates a spiritual practice of attentiveness to how one feels and following it while interacting with one's chosen instrument. Developing an awareness of one's mental and emotional state informs not only one's act of creating but one's awareness of themselves: why they feel the way they do, and how they can express it through this creative form.

Artistic practices of all kinds serve both as methods of self-expression and of emotional release. The better attuned we are to what is happening inside of us as we play, paint, draw, write, and so on, the more in touch we are both with our chosen medium and with ourselves.

Along with attentiveness to our own emotional responses to the world around us comes attentiveness to what God is trying to say to us or how God is present with us. Just as we are discovering ourselves in creative actions, we are also expressing God's creativity that resides within us. Spiritual director William Barry notes that when we experience God's creative touch, "we are talking about an action of God that is going on continually, not one that happened in some distant point in time."[4]

To create is to experience an intersection of our own self-realization and God's creative spark continually manifesting through our gifts. We may be novices just learning how to use a paintbrush or a set of knitting needles or we may be more experienced practitioners of our chosen craft. Regardless, we are faced with the opportunity to bring beauty into the world just as God first did, is doing, and chooses to do through us, as well as consider our own mood and mindset as we do it.

Have you ever sat down to draw, sing, or cut a block of wood and before you know it, several hours have passed? Have you ever become so lost in your chosen creative outlet, so locked into what you are doing, that you are able to forget the world around you in order to become one with the creative process? Have you ever noticed an inward movement of joy or sadness or anger that your work seems to inspire? In those times, have you ever chosen to let it guide you as you're creating? Or have you been moved to stop for a moment to let such emotions happen to you completely before continuing?

Such moments during times of creating can be times to wonder at what is happening, both in terms of questioning where it comes from, but also in taking it with awe, having found yourself in the current and allowing it to move you downstream into a new understanding of God's presence and of yourself. Just as we read in Genesis 1 that God rested on the seventh day of creation, we too could stop for a moment and perhaps even utter an "amen."

One year during the season of Lent, a 40-day period before Easter that many Christians use to prepare and reflect before this celebration of resurrection, I decided to spend that time writing a song. I have what I'll call a moderate amount of musical skill, and my spiritual practice during this season would be to compose something using my acoustic guitar. The only criteria that I set for myself was that I just needed to work on the song for a little while every day. If I came up with a single word for the lyrics or just strummed the chorus a few times, if I worked with it for two minutes or for a half hour, it didn't matter so long as I did something every day.

During this particular year, Lent fell right in the middle of a career transition for me. I was changing churches, having finished my time at one to begin anew at another. This significant life change inevitably made its way into my songwriting, because while I was trying to create this piece I was also attempting to work through all the emotions of leaving a place and a group of people I'd known for so long while also attempting to become acclimated to a new place and group.

The first week or so of this exercise mostly had to do with chord progression and song structure as I tried to figure out what the song would sound like. Then, as I began working on the lyrics, it turned out that the song ended up reflecting the transition I was experiencing. I wrote about how no one place has been my home for very long, but also how I end up making home of my latest destination as I settle in with the geography, culture, and people given enough time.

While I never consciously prayed during my time of creativity, I could sense God's presence at various points as I worked through my own internal experience of change and its accompanying swirl of emotions. I used the creative skills I had as a prayerful act that involved healing, anticipation, adjustment, lament, thankfulness, and excitement for a new adventure.

Creating had helped me go with the current of my heart, allowing it to carry me into a new space both internally and externally. I'd made use of the creative spark placed within me by God, letting it lead the way to bring something new into the world, just as God had done with me. As with my carefully crafted communion set, I'd infused my song with prayer even if I wasn't always aware I was doing it.

PRAYER EXERCISE AND QUESTIONS FOR REFLECTION

1. Identify the creative outlet that is most exhilarating and meaningful for you, whether a form of artistic expression, working with your hands, building, or whatever else. Reflect on why this activity is meaningful for you, how long you've been doing it, who you've learned from to develop it, and so on.

2. Set aside a block of time each day to work with your chosen creative outlet. Decide first whether you will do this for a week, two weeks, a month, or longer. Don't worry if you'll only be able to spend a few minutes on it during certain days, or whether you'll have a finished product to show for it by the end. The act of creating in itself is the important part.

3. As you sit down to create each time during your chosen period, begin with a brief prayer for God to guide you as you work. Prepare to focus on creating and let your prayer hang over your creativity without dwelling on it.

4. Pay attention to your thoughts and feelings as you work. What is guiding you as you create? What are you hung up on? Are you working through a negative emotion such as despair or anger? Note how you feel by the time you're finished for the day as opposed to when you started.

5. When you end your time, reflect on how God may have been a part of your creating. Did you lose track of time? Were you at any point overcome with emotion due to what you're making? Did you experience any forward movement in something in your life you've been wrestling with?

6. Conclude your creative time with an acknowledgment of God's presence, whether a simple "thank you" or "amen" or something longer if desired. Set down your work until the next day.

NOTES

[1] Michael Ivens. *Understanding the Spiritual Exercises.* (Herefordshire: Gracewing, 1998), 29

[2] William Barry. *Letting God Come Close.* (Chicago: Loyola, 2001), 58.

[3] Victor Wooten. *The Music Lesson.* (New York: Berkley, 2006), 109.

[4] Barry, 62.

10

WHILE SERVING

*a*s a pastor, I've taught confirmation quite often. For the unfamiliar, many mainline Protestant Christian traditions offer a regular program for youth—usually around middle school age—to learn more about topics related to church and faith leading up to their becoming official members of the church. Other traditions have similar processes that go by other names and you may have memories of going through such a time of education and preparation yourself.

For years, I required my confirmation classes to do a service project. I wanted them to have some sense that being a person of faith included a component of helping others, of coming to the aid of those who for many reasons are going through a difficult time. My own experiences being raised in churches impressed this on me through summer mission trips and other opportunities for people to come together and offer what resources we could to ease people's burdens.

Another local church in our area housed a food pantry that our church and others supported through a community ministerial association of which we were members. Around Thanksgiving and Christmas, the pantry would organize an evening of packing boxes of food to be delivered to area families who otherwise wouldn't be able to provide meals for themselves during these holiday times. I saw this as an easy way to have my confirmation students fulfill the service requirement, as well as to lend our tangible assistance to an area ministry that we supported through other means throughout the year.

We entered the church's basement that first year unsure of what to expect. The room was full of shelves and tables covered in non-perishable food organized by type, with the actual packing of boxes consisting of each of us receiving a checklist of items that we'd have to go around and collect. Once we located every item we'd take our box to a designated spot to be marked for distribution.

Before any of that began, however, the youth pastor of the church quieted the group to read scripture and offer communion. He set the mood and the context for us that evening by reminding us that just as Jesus fed the first disciples during his meal with them prior to his death, so we are tasked with doing what we can to provide food for others. He was not content to let this be a time to pack a few boxes and do some nice things for people during the holiday season. Instead, he wanted to frame what we were doing as part of our calling as disciples.

For people of faith, service has a spiritual dimension as well as a physical one. How good are we at remembering that?

SPIRITUALITY AND SERVICE: HOPELESSLY LINKED

For some, finding time to serve is just as difficult as finding time to pray or to exercise. Dedicating oneself to help at a food pantry or soup kitchen means devoting hours out of one's week to doing that and not something else. It means another item on the calendar, complete with commute to and from the agency offering the assistance to those in need. Even the thought of committing to service in this way might cause people to feel exhausted given everything else they might already be involved in.

Fortunately for these people, churches and other places do offer ways to help that require a much lower amount of energy. One might not be able to show up to an agency of some kind, but that box in the lobby calling for cans of food is pretty easy. The person outside the grocery store with the kettle of change around Christmas just wants whatever coins you have in your pocket. All dropping off used clothing at a thrift store requires is a few minutes' drive and dumping some boxes by a door.

Whether this is what Jesus really intended for his disciples is an open question. True enough, people need food, money, and clothing. But God also invites us to consider whether these acts are enough. How much of a connection do we really make with the people we're serving by throwing a can of soup in a box? Or by giving shirts we've deemed too small, too unfashionable, or too worn out to a thrift shop?

If we were in the position of those we want to help, would we want the help we're giving?

Other people of faith may have a different issue when it comes to service. In certain theological circles, the thought of spending the time and energy to consider the true spiritual reasons why we are serving is a waste of time. Who has time to pray when people need houses built, or a decent meal, or support as they advocate for their rights?

Even while considering themselves Christians, some exhibit hostility toward slowing down to think about why they feel called to do what they're doing. In the story above, they may have questioned why we were standing around sharing communion when boxes of food needed to be packed. *We'll talk about what Jesus thinks about this later*, they might have said. *Right now, let's get to work.*

In different ways, each of these approaches shows a disconnect between spirituality and service. The former acknowledges that God wants them to do good for others, but engages in a token, symbolic gesture hoping that it's enough. The latter is focused on doing good, with a vague intent of coming up with some theological reasoning for it after the fact.

You may fall into one of these categories, and if that is the case I'll say two things. First, you have the desire and are in your own way already participating in some form of service. But you may also be wondering how to deepen either your commitment to doing something or your understanding of why you're doing it. Both intentions are worth nurturing and will lead to a better sense of how the two are connected.

Second, for people of faith in particular, cultivating a deeper sense of God in one's life—whether through prayer, study, worship, or some other spiritual practice—is meant to lead to service. Actions such as feeding the hungry, donating resources to places that offer assistance, or becoming involved in activist work on behalf of others is meant to be a natural outgrowth of a relationship with God. Such a relationship includes a calling, and service is a response to that calling. Each leads to and deepens one's understanding of the other.

Spirituality and service are linked. Christians can attempt to do just one, but it would not lead to the fullness of life and depth of prayerful experience that God intends for us.

JESUS WITH THE SUFFERING

Near the end of the Gospel of Matthew, Jesus presents a vision meant to help his listeners understand that service is more than just an option. And the reason he gives is spiritual as much as moral.

> When the Son of Man comes in his glory, and all the angels with him, then he will sit on the throne of his glory. [32]All the nations will be gathered before him, and he will separate people one from another as a shepherd separates the sheep from the goats, [33]and he

will put the sheep at his right hand and the goats at the left.
[34]Then the king will say to those at his right hand, 'Come, you
that are blessed by my Father, inherit the kingdom prepared for
you from the foundation of the world; [35]for I was hungry and you
gave me food, I was thirsty and you gave me something to drink, I
was a stranger and you welcomed me, [36]I was naked and you gave
me clothing, I was sick and you took care of me, I was in prison
and you visited me.' [37]Then the righteous will answer him, 'Lord,
when was it that we saw you hungry and gave you food, or thirsty
and gave you something to drink? [38]And when was it that we saw
you a stranger and welcomed you, or naked and gave you
clothing? [39]And when was it that we saw you sick or in prison and
visited you?' [40]And the king will answer them, 'Truly I tell you,
just as you did it to one of the least of these who are members of
my family, you did it to me.' [41]Then he will say to those at his left
hand, 'You that are accursed, depart from me into the eternal fire
prepared for the devil and his angels; [42]for I was hungry and you
gave me no food, I was thirsty and you gave me nothing to drink,
[43]I was a stranger and you did not welcome me, naked and you
did not give me clothing, sick and in prison and you did not visit
me.' [44]Then they also will answer, 'Lord, when was it that we saw
you hungry or thirsty or a stranger or naked or sick or in prison,
and did not take care of you?' [45]Then he will answer them, 'Truly I
tell you, just as you did not do it to one of the least of these, you
did not do it to me.' [46]And these will go away into eternal
punishment, but the righteous into eternal life. (Matthew
25:31-46)

This vision that Jesus presents might be discomfiting for
several reasons. The first is that he is painting a picture of a
scenario of final judgment, which might make a lot of people—
believer and non-believer alike—nervous. After all, who wants to
talk about such things in polite company? Second, the criteria that
the Son of Man seems to be using for separation and sentence is

based less on belief and more on ethical action. Through what he says here, he cares much less whether people got their theology right and more whether they helped those in need.

The setup is simple: the Son of Man arrives with a chorus of angels to gather "all the nations" together. The term "all nations" does not refer to recognized governments and the people they represent, but all people from the entire earth as individuals and without commonly understood boundaries. To the Son of Man, such national identity is not important and doesn't serve the purpose of this gathering.[1]

The Son of Man separates this large assembly into two groups, like a shepherd separating sheep and goats. He turns to the first group and invites them into the divine kingdom because they saw him hungry, thirsty, lonely, in prison, sick, or naked, and provided the appropriate and necessary help in those instances. This series of statements comes as a shock to the people, as they have no recollection of ever doing such things for him and ask, "When did we see you in need in all these different ways and help you?" The Son of Man responds with the theological heart of the story: "Whenever you did it to the least of these who are my family, you did it to me" (Matthew 25:40).

This statement has several possible meanings, although it has a primary thrust that is more universal. Jesus may be speaking in general terms, where a moment of serving others is a moment of serving him, no matter the specifics of the person being helped. Others cite the inclusion of the phrase "who are members of my family" and suggest that it means a disciple's primary concern should be for fellow members of the church. So what does he mean by this; how are we to interpret this for ourselves?

M. Eugene Boring suggests that regardless of specific interpretation preferences, the primary purpose of this story is to address human need.[2] Jesus presents the strong implication that when one sees somebody in need of relief in some way, responding to that need is what he desires. To take it a step further, he states that to feed the hungry, clothe the naked, and care for the sick is to feed, clothe, and care for Jesus himself; that he is present in the hurting people of this world, and compassionate action is the fitting response to that presence. Whether one chooses to focus this response on people inside or outside the church is a secondary concern, so long as you're doing it at all.

This vision combines faith and service in a way that helps us recognize that both are important. The first group may have been doing what they thought was right on its own merits, but there was a pervasive underlying spiritual reality to what they were doing, even if they weren't always or ever aware of it.

The overall point of this vision, however, is that we are meant to be aware of it and act out of that awareness. Jesus is incarnate in human need, and to serve people in pain and hoping for relief is to serve the one who is suffering in love with them.

SEEING JESUS EVERYWHERE

Some of my most memorable and treasured service experiences happened in inner-city Philadelphia. I was part of several short-term mission trips where we stayed at Old First Reformed Church in one of its downtown neighborhoods. The church has an extensive relationship with area ministries to the homeless population, and we spent any given day in soup kitchens, sorting clothes at a thrift store, and hanging out with those living in shelters to hear their stories. During my high school and college years, these experiences were influential and formative in my own sense of how important and inseparable mission and service is to a life of faith.

At the end of every day, my group would come together in Old First's sanctuary to process our experiences, share what we've learned, and pray. The way our leader would always frame the conversation was to ask, "Where did you see Jesus today?" She wanted us to think deeper than "How did you help?" or "What difference do you think you made today?" She pushed us to consider the presence of God with those we met or helped; to think about how these ways of serving were not to make us feel good about ourselves or to help for helping's own sake. Rather, we were to think about the connection between faith and service— that one leads to the other because it is so central to what Jesus called his disciples to do.

Our culture is one that prefers easy solutions and convenient methods, and people of faith are just as susceptible to the temptation to act first and think later. The need around us on those trips was obvious, as are the volume of needs that surround us every day. It may be that you are aware of such needs in your own community or have a strong passion about larger issues of discrimination, poverty, or ignorance that run deeper or wider than your area alone. These needs may seem so urgent that there's no time to consider the theological implications or the nature of God's call to people of faith to respond to them. Maybe we can do that later, after hours, when a day's work is complete and someone's burden has been eased even a little.

"Where did you see Jesus today?" is a crucial question to ask. It helps people of faith consider the spiritual dimension of what they feel called to do for others. An equally important and helpful question is, "Where do you see Jesus now?" There are days when thinking about Jesus' presence within the world's aches and anxieties might be better for *us*. We'd be able to consider such things with clear heads away from the noise and distractions of the moment.

But that spiritual dimension extends to the present moment, the one that brings wonder and frustration and sadness and guilt. It extends to the moment when you're standing in the grocery store considering whether to buy a few extra cans of green beans for the box at your church. It extends to the moment when a man asks you for spare change on the street. It extends to hours spent preparing a meal or joining a demonstration in front of your statehouse.

Jesus is there, right now, with those who need basic sustenance and advocacy. What difference might it make to remember that *as* you serve, rather than after the fact? What if we considered how every moment is a time of communion with God and God's beloved?

PRAYER PRACTICE AND QUESTIONS FOR REFLECTION

1. Identify some way you would like to serve or are currently serving, whether through your faith community, a civic organization you're a part of, or something you do with your family or on your own. Think about the reasons that draw you to this particular cause or action: do you have personal ties to it, or does it simply fit your schedule better than other options? Why did you get involved or why would you want to become involved in this project?

2. Think about the role that God's calling plays in your desire to serve in this way. How have you acknowledged God in choosing to give your time and energy to this action, or how would you like to be more intentional in acknowledging God in this way?

3. Think about the people you are helping. How do you experience the presence of God as you share your gifts, resources, and time with others? How do you think Jesus is with the hungry, thirsty, stranger, naked, and imprisoned in your area? What difference do you believe it makes to consider those in need in this way?

4. Return to the Matthew story mentioned in this chapter. In the coming week, adopt a practice of praying "Jesus, help me see you in them" as you go about your daily schedule. Recite it during your commute before you get to work, as your household wakes

up in the morning, as you head to evening activities, and as you participate in service projects. Try to keep in active thought how Jesus is with those experiencing happiness, heartbreak, setbacks, or anxiety. How might you be called to respond to the Jesus in them?

NOTES

[1] M. Eugene Boring, "The Gospel of Matthew," from *The New Interpreter's Bible, Vol. VIII* (Nashville: Abingdon, 1995), 456.

[2] *Ibid.*, 456.

11

PERMISSION TO MOVE

These days I don't often drum on tabletops the way I did in 5th grade. I may play a quick cadence on my legs here and there, but as a method of releasing nervous energy, I've left many of my old school band tendencies behind. It may be that my routines of stretching in the morning, coupled with regular exercise, have eliminated the need, but I don't think that is really the case. After all, much like my strong urge to walk the labyrinth at that retreat center rather than sit down to my prayer book, I can't say that I've yet mastered the art of sitting still, and I probably never will.

Around the time my first child was born, I began a habit of shifting my weight from one leg to the other, resulting in a slow swaying motion when standing. Sure, in those days there were many hours spent rocking a tiny human in my arms trying to get him to calm down or fall asleep. And many, when they noticed me doing it even without holding a baby, concluded that that's what started it, and even if I'm not trying to comfort a child my body has become so used to the movement that I've taken to doing it any time.

But I don't think that was it. I do trace this fidgety action back to around that same time, but I associate it more with explicitly spiritual moments than parenting ones. At the first church I pastored, I took to standing by the entrance to the sanctuary to greet everyone walking in, and at some point began rocking from one foot to the other while waiting for more hands to shake. This same motion would begin during the silence leading up to my giving the pastoral prayer on behalf of the congregation, and while reading off requests handed to me by the ushers. I've even had one church member request that I never stop doing it while praying, as it provides some form of comfort for parishioners as they participate as well.

So I've been given permission to move while I pray. And I hope that over the course of this book you have realized that you have such permission as well. Not only do you have permission, in fact, but there are ways to pray in the midst of doing other things, because those moments and places are just as sacred and infused with God's presence as sitting in a church sanctuary or spending time at a retreat center.

Why is that? Because God cares about how you're feeling at work. God is concerned with your times of running the family around to different places. God created your body and is as concerned with its health as you are. God is with you on your morning walk and in your bedroom while you fold laundry and while you're driving to your favorite getaway spot.

You're on the move so often, and it's not that you have to sit still finally to find God. Instead, you can recognize God in the midst of what you're already doing.

JACOB AND A MOVING GOD

In the book of Genesis, Jacob is introduced as one of the great ancestors of the people of Israel. But he doesn't seem so great in many of the stories about him contained in this part of the Bible. He tricks his older brother Esau into giving him his birthright for a bowl of soup, and later he tricks his father Isaac into giving him the patriarchal blessing, again meant for his older brother.

You can imagine that after such events, Esau didn't think much of his younger brother, and you'd be correct. By the time Jacob hears word that Esau is coming to meet him in Genesis 29, part of this message is that his brother is bringing a small army with him. Considering everything that he's put Esau through, Jacob is fearing that his chickens are coming home to roost, and he sends his family across the river Jabbok ahead of him for their safety while he stays behind. At that point, a curious encounter happens.

> Jacob was left alone; and a man wrestled with him until daybreak. [25]When the man saw that he did not prevail against Jacob, he struck him on the hip socket; and Jacob's hip was put out of joint as he wrestled with him. [26]Then he said, "Let me go, for the day is breaking." But Jacob said, "I will not let you go, unless you bless me." [27]So he said to him, "What is your name?" And he said, "Jacob." [28]Then the man said, "You shall no longer be called Jacob, but Israel, for you have striven with God and with humans, and have prevailed." [29]Then Jacob asked him, "Please tell me your name." But he said, "Why is it that you ask my name?" And there he blessed him. (Genesis 32:24-29)

This may be a strange Biblical story with which to wrap things up, but consider what happens in terms of the unexpected way Jacob seems to have a divine experience. He is at an especially low point, close to facing down his own flesh and blood, who has more than one grievance and, many would argue, more than one cause for retribution. While considering this reunion and all that it may bring, Jacob is also facing down his mortality and his actions of selfishness and greed that brought him to this point.

Imagine being so beside yourself, so worked up by your own thoughts and past actions. Recall moments when you've been kept awake by something you've done or something that someone else has done to you perhaps years or even decades earlier, even something that you thought you'd already resolved for yourself. Remember how such thoughts affect your body, causing tension in your muscles and tightness in your stomach.

This is what Jacob is experiencing, perhaps pacing the riverbank, maybe even muttering to himself as he attempts to figure out how to receive his brother once he arrives. Sitting still probably wasn't an option; his nerves wouldn't allow him.

And yet he ends up encountering God here, and in a way befitting his predicament: he finds himself not just wrestling with all that he's done and all that might be coming for him, but he is in a literal wrestling match with an unknown figure. They seem to be on equal footing, as their bout lasts the entire night without either claiming a clear upper hand, until the unnamed opponent realizes that it's close to daybreak and he needs to go.

At this point, Jacob clamps on a side headlock and refuses to let go until his adversary blesses him, to which this mystery figure agrees. Jacob is renamed Israel, which means "wrestles with God," suggesting that this challenger is divine in nature.

We struggle with our past actions, and with what has been done to us. We struggle to keep our schedules straight when we and our loved ones seem pulled in so many individual directions every day. We struggle to stay on task at work while also keeping a workout regimen. We struggle to stay focused during long stretches of time and to sit still when our bodies want to do otherwise.

And so many struggle with prayer. We struggle to fit it into our days and with how to do it once we can, when there's so much else we're concerned about. And at a deeper level, beyond any particular practice, we may struggle with our relationship with God, wondering how God is a part of any of these other parts of our lives or how we might tap into that presence and deepen our understanding of it.

Like Jacob, we may be incapable of sitting still, too fidgety and frantic to notice how God is calling attention to God's presence in our lives. We may pace just on the edge of awareness, striving to bring it to the forefront of our thoughts so we might receive the blessing of knowing how God is with us. Our prayer life, such as it is, might be better characterized as a constant time of wrestling as we seek what to do, how to do it, and what God might be speaking into our lives without our realizing. And our minds might be too busy, our bodies too squirmy, our day-planners too full.

Many of us are in need of ways to pray through our struggles other than sitting still, because our struggles might not allow us that level of quiet. And so my prayer for those who have picked up this book is twofold.

First, I pray that you are able to be honest with yourself about what those struggles are. Whatever combination of regret, busyness, preoccupation, overstimulation, and anxiety you are facing, I hope that you are first able to be honest with yourself about all of it, and about what you need to do to work toward a life that features greater balance that includes addressing and incorporating spiritual wellness into the whole of who you are.

Second, I pray that whatever you believe is keeping you from finding time to nurture that part of yourself, something in this book will help you identify ways to change that. Whatever keeps you pacing at the riverbank, I hope that you will be able to find some way to alter that through new practices that will develop into new habits, and that those new habits will nurture a continual realization of what was always true: God is with you even in the hustle and bustle of your daily life, loving and blessing you through it all.

PRAYER AT ALL HOURS

This chapter began with a description of my nervous habit of swaying while I stand. It came in handy with my firstborn, but it correlated with that important life moment rather than being caused by it. By the time my second child was born, I took on a new understanding of what that habit could be.

Our children are five years apart. That means that around the time our son turned a year old, we enjoyed about four years of nights uninterrupted by crying due to a small child needing to be fed or to have their diaper changed. When our daughter was born, most of these tasks came back to us like putting on a comfortable shoe. That is to say that we were well-acquainted with what to do and how best to do it, but with those needed tasks also came occasional and familiar feelings of frustration brought about by elusive sleep and the cries of a restless infant.

I did a lot of swaying during those nights, as well as a lot of pacing and patting the small of my newborn's back in efforts to soothe her back to silence. In my more self-aware moments during these early hours, I also took to praying while I rocked. I'd pray for myself, just to keep my emotions in check and to focus on the needs at hand. I'd pray for my daughter, that she'd find peace and comfort from whatever was causing her to be upset. I'd pray for the rest of my family as we continued to navigate this transition from three members to four.

I was like Jacob wrestling with God on the riverbank in the middle of the night, praying my way through the hours, seeking a blessing for the two of us, and trying to find how God was with us as we swayed along together. I couldn't set her down in order pluck up a devotional book, and "being still" wasn't going to do either of us any good. So I needed a different way of acknowledging the divine presence as we struggled and strove for rest.

I admit that I'm still not able to convert each difficult or busy moment into one of prayer and centering; I am on the same imperfect journey as everyone else in that regard. But I have seen that it's possible, and I want you to know that it's possible for your own life as well. Whether you're loading the dishwasher, enjoying a meal with loved ones, waiting on the train for your stop to arrive, soldering pipes during your shift at the factory, or trying to rock a baby to sleep before dawn, these times can be prayerful. And the reason for that is God is already there.

You are moving, and God is moving with you, and there are ways to connect these two truths for a more whole and holy way to view the world. You have permission to move, and to pray while you do it.

CPSIA information can be obtained
at www.ICGtesting.com
Printed in the USA
FSHW01n0819240918
52490FS